Kids Can Press

The J ... ian
Cookbook

Kids Can Press
The Jumbo Vegetarian
Cookbook

Written by
Judi Gillies and
Jennifer Glossop

Illustrated by
Louise Phillips

Kids Can Press

Kids Can Press acknowledges the financial support of the Government of Canada, through the BPIDP, for our publishing activity.

Published in Canada by
Kids Can Press Ltd.
29 Birch Avenue
Toronto, ON M4V 1E2

Published in the U.S. by
Kids Can Press Ltd.
2250 Military Road
Tonawanda, NY 14150

www.kidscanpress.com

Edited by Shaun Oakey
Designed by Marie Bartholomew

Front cover and right back cover model photo by Ray Boudreau
Left back cover model photo by Frank Baldassarra

Printed and bound in Canada

CM PA 02 0 9 8 7 6 5 4 3 2 1

National Library of Canada Cataloguing in Publication Data

Gillies, Judi

   The jumbo vegetarian cookbook

(Kids Can Press jumbo book series)
Includes index.
ISBN 1-55074-477-3

   1. Vegetarian cookery — Juvenile literature. I. Glossop, Jennifer II. Phillips, Louise III. Title. IV. Series.

TX837.G55 2002   j641.5'636   C2001-900488-7

Kids Can Press is a Nelvana company

 Acknowledgments

We would like to thank our daughters, Erica Glossop and Emma Gillies, for bringing vegetarianism home and for inspiring this book by their commitment to a vegetarian diet and lifestyle. Many of the recipes are theirs or were developed with their help. For assistance in the kitchen and for tasting and testing, we'd also like to thank Eden Levinsky, Jenny Brown, Patty Talbot, Alison Atyeo, Paul Lagos, Susan Gillies, Marlene Danicki and our families, especially John Glossop and Michael Gillies.

   Liz Pearson, author and nutritionist, made extremely helpful suggestions about nutrition for vegetarians. Our editor, Shaun Oakey, proved that he is the most knowledgeable and tactful cookbook editor around. And to everyone at Kids Can Press, thanks for letting us explore the delights and rewards of vegetarian cooking for and with kids.

Judi Gillies and
Jennifer Glossop

Contents

⭐ Vegetables

⭐ Sauces and Fillings

⭐ Cookies and Desserts

⭐ Drinks

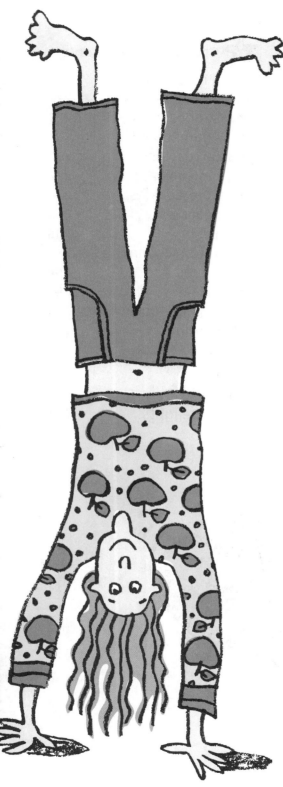

Welcome to the Kitchen!

Emma Gillies loves taking care of animals. Growing up, she looked after the family pets: a dog, a couple of cats and a bird. She worried about other animals, too, especially when she read about how farm animals are raised. Her family wasn't surprised, therefore, when she decided to stop eating meat. "I didn't become a vegetarian for my health," she said. "I did it for the health of the chickens and cows."

Erica Glossop also loves animals and became a pesco-vegetarian when she was a teenager. In grade seven, Erica had learned that a farm that grows plants can feed more people than one the same size that raises animals for food. When Erica stopped eating meat, she knew she was helping the environment. She knew that other people changed their diets for health reasons, and still others had religious reasons not to eat meat.

As Emma's and Erica's mothers, we worried at first that plants alone would not give them everything their growing bodies needed. They reassured us that they would eat a wide variety of foods and learn all they could about their new choices. We also knew they both loved to cook and would prepare many of their own meals.

Since then, both our families have learned a lot. Erica and Emma have introduced us to great food, like tempeh kabobs and bean salads. We've also found ways to make veggie versions of our old family standbys, like shepherd's pie, and we've discovered dishes like baked tofu or lentil loaf that they can cook when everyone else is having meat.

If you have decided to switch to a vegetarian diet, or are thinking of doing so, you're part of a growing group of people who have chosen not to eat meat, fish or poultry. There's nothing new about vegetarianism. Many famous people in the past, such as Albert Einstein, Mahatma Gandhi and George Bernard Shaw, advocated a vegetarian diet. And nowadays lots of popular actors and singers, like Paul McCartney and Madonna, promote a healthy meat-free diet.

We hope this book will help you find foods that fit your new eating plan. Here, you'll find breakfasts, lunches, dinners, snacks and treats — all family tested and approved. If you're just getting started, choose the beginner recipes, or ask for help with the intermediate or advanced ones. If you're an old hand in the kitchen, use our menus to make complete meals for every day and for special occasions.

Have fun with the recipes. Be creative. Be daring. Being the chef means that you get to cook foods that you like the way you like them. When you do the cooking, you get to make your own choices, and that's what being a vegetarian is all about.

What Kind of Vegetarian Are You?

All vegetarians eat plants, but some eat other things as well:

▷ Lacto-ovo vegetarians eat dairy products — milk (*lacto*) and foods made from milk, like cheese and butter — and eggs (*ovo*). If someone eats eggs but not dairy, she or he is an ovo-vegetarian. Dairy but not eggs? That would be a lacto-vegetarian.

▷ Vegans (pronounced VEE-gans by some and VAY-gans by others) eat no animal products — no meat, eggs or dairy products. Many also stay away from honey (made by bees), leather (made from the skin of animals), silk (made by silk worms) and down (the feathers of ducks and geese).

▷ Some vegetarians eat fish. They are pesco-vegetarians. Others called pollo-vegetarians eat chicken but no red meat. Which is the best? It's up to you, although the more you leave out, the more care you need to take to make sure your diet is healthy.

Plants, Plants and More Plants

All food — even meat — began with plants. Cows eat grass, chickens eat grains and many fish eat tiny sea plants. Some of the biggest animals — think of whales and giraffes — are vegetarians, and so were many towering dinosaurs, like *Brontosaurus*. But animals have to eat their veggies raw, usually fresh from a tree. We have lots more choices — and we can cook and spice up our plants in lots of different ways.

Let's look at some of the plants — and parts of plants — that you can choose from.

 Leaves

Some leaves are best eaten raw or in salads — lettuce of all kinds, spinach, arugula and so on. Other leaves are best cooked — kale, collard greens, bok choy. The darker the green, the more vitamins they contain. If some of these foods are new to you, visit a grocery store and check out all the leafy choices.

Roots and tubers

Carrots, turnips, parsnips, yams and sweet potatoes are the roots of plants. Tubers, like potatoes, grow on the roots. Not only are they great for you, they last a long time in the fridge or cupboard.

Seeds

Plants make seeds so that new plants can grow. Seeds are like a package of food to feed the young plant.

Seeds come in lots of edible forms:

▷ Nuts — Nuts are seeds with a hard coating. Nuts can be eaten plain as a snack or added to other foods like granola, stews, stir-fries or desserts. You can add nuts to all sorts of dishes — walnuts to salads, sunflower seeds or almonds to granola. Some nuts can be made into pastes such as almond butter to be spread on toast and bread, or tahini, which is made from sesame seeds, to add to stews and sauces.

▶ Sprouts — Sprouts are seeds that have started to grow just a bit. They add crunch to salads, sandwiches and wraps and extra vitamins to your diet.

▶ Corn — Corn is native to North America and is used in Mexican and Native American cooking. Corn on the cob is a summertime favorite. Corn kernels from a can or scraped off the cob can be added to chilies and soups. Ground-up corn (cornmeal) goes into breads, tortillas and polenta.

▶ Fruits — Apples, pears, plums, mangoes and more. You can eat the sweet part that covers these seeds raw for a snack, raw or cooked as dessert, or added to soups, salads or main dishes. Some fruits — like tomatoes and peppers — are called vegetables. All fruits are packed with vitamins and energy.

▶ Grains — Grains — such as wheat, rye, barley, oats and rice — are the seeds of grasses. Around the world they are a basic food. In Asia, rice feeds millions of people. In Europe and North America, bread made from wheat is eaten for breakfast, lunch and dinner. Not all bread comes in loaves. There are also flat breads like pita from the Middle East, chapatis from India, rotis from the West Indies and focaccia from Italy. Pasta — spaghetti and all its relatives — is also made from wheat and from other grains. Grains provide energy and vitamins galore. Try some that you might not be as familiar with, such as buckwheat, kamut (pronounced kah-MOOT), spelt and quinoa (pronounced KEEN-wa). These grains and others can be cooked and eaten as cereal or made into flour for baking.

▶ Beans — Beans are seeds in a pod. Some beans — like green and yellow beans or peas — are cooked fresh or frozen, with or without their pod. Others — like black beans, soybeans and kidney beans — are dried and then cooked. These beans are also called legumes, and it's hard to imagine a vegetarian diet without them. They fill you up, they taste great, and they provide a good source of protein. Try kidney beans in chili, black beans in soup and salads, chickpeas (garbanzo beans) in hummus and salads. Legumes come dried or cooked in cans. Our recipes call for the canned kind since they are quicker and easier to cook with.

nutrition

Some people worry that not eating meat makes it harder to stay healthy and get all the nutrients your body requires. Don't worry. A vegetarian diet can easily provide all the good things you need to grow up strong. Eat all those plant parts — especially nuts, seeds and beans — in lots of ways, and you'll be fine. And if you drink milk and eat yogurt, cheese and eggs, you'll find it easier to get all the nutrients you need. If you are worried, however, check with a health practitioner or nutritionist to make sure you're eating right.

 Three kinds of food

Scientists like to divide foods into carbohydrates, fats and proteins. You need some of each to stay in good health, have lots of energy and grow strong.

▷ Carbohydrates give you energy. It's easy to get enough carbohydrates since they are found in fruits and vegetables, beans, bread, cereal and pasta.

▷ Fats help your body run properly and give you energy. Some fats are healthier than others. You can get fat from vegetables and vegetable oils. However, one healthy kind of fat is common in fish but not in plants. It's called omega-3 and is also found in flaxseed oil and walnuts.

▷ Our bodies need protein. Proteins are made up of building blocks called amino acids. Our bodies make some of these amino acids, but we get the others — called the essential proteins — only from the food we eat. Meat, eggs, dairy products and soybeans contain all the essential proteins, but other plants contain only some. It used to be thought that you had to eat all the essential proteins together at the same meal — for example, beans and rice, which together have all the essential proteins. You do need all those essential proteins, but you don't need to eat them together. For example, if you eat beans for lunch and rice for dinner, you will still get all the essential proteins.

 Vitamins and minerals

In addition to carbohydrates, fats and protein, food provides us with vitamins and minerals that make our bodies run well. Here are some of the most important:

▷ Vitamins A and C — These important vitamins, which, among other things, keep you from getting sick, are found in lots of plants, especially fruits and vegetables.

▷ Vitamin D — If you spend time in the sun, you'll get lots of this vitamin, which along with calcium gives you strong bones and teeth. If not, look for foods like milk and orange juice that are fortified with vitamin D, or take a multivitamin.

▶ B Vitamins — Grains are loaded with these.

▶ Vitamin B_{12} — This vitamin helps your body use the food you eat. If you don't eat eggs or milk products (all of which contain B_{12}), look for cereals that are fortified with B_{12} or take a vitamin supplement.

▶ Iron — Iron helps your red blood cells. This mineral is found in beans, molasses, raisins and dark green vegetables. Your body uses the iron in these foods better if you eat them with a food that contains vitamin C, such as orange juice, peppers or kiwis.

▶ Calcium — Calcium makes bones and teeth strong and is especially important for growing young people. Milk and other dairy products contain lots of calcium. If you don't eat them, or don't eat enough, you can top up your calcium supply with vegetables like kale, collard greens and okra, and with tofu, soy milk or orange juice that are fortified with calcium (check the labels).

Those amazing soybeans

If you eat Asian food, you are likely already familiar with food made from soybeans. This nutritious bean is becoming more common in North American cooking.

Soybeans aren't usually eaten plain, but you will find them in lots of other places. Here are some of the foods made from soy.

▶ Soy milk — Soy milk is a liquid made from cooked and strained soybeans. It makes a refreshing drink, and if it is fortified, it can be used as a substitute for cow's milk on cereal or in baking.

▶ Tofu — Tofu (pronounced TOE-foo) doesn't have much flavor of its own, but it soaks up other tastes and can be delicious. It is made from soy milk that is thickened and pressed into cakes. Tofu comes in different thicknesses: soft, firm and extra-firm. You can make it firmer and more absorbent by pressing out the water. (Place it in a colander or on towels, cover and place a weight on top.) For a chewier texture, freeze then thaw tofu. Silken tofu, which has a smooth soft texture, comes in sealed packages. Check all tofu packages for instructions on storing and for an expiry date. Open tofu should be kept in fresh water in the fridge. Change the water every day or so. Tofu should smell fresh.

▶ Miso — Miso (ME-so) is soybean paste. It is used in soups, dressings and sauces.

▶ Tempeh — Tempeh (TEM-pay) looks like a cake of pressed beans, which is exactly what it is. It can be made into a wonderful-tasting, chewy food. Cut it into chunks, marinate it and use it like meat in stir-fries, stews, kabobs and soups.

▶ TVP (textured vegetable protein) — This soy product is made from soy flour that is pressed into granules. It looks like dry bread crumbs, but when you add water, it puffs up and takes on the texture of ground meat. It absorbs other flavors and can be used as a substitute for hamburger in dishes like tacos and shepherd's pie. It comes in plastic bags or loose in bulk stores.

Before You Start

The recipes in all cookbooks leave some things out. It would take too long — and get too boring — to tell you every time to wash your hands or to use oven mitts when touching something hot, so we just assume you know that.

There are some other things that we won't tell you each time but that you should know. Before you begin to cook:

▷ Read the recipe all the way through.
▷ Get all the ingredients and utensils that you will need.
▷ Rinse any fruits and vegetables.
▷ Cut, chop or slice all the ingredients that need it.
▷ Measure the ingredients.
▷ Oh, yes — don't forget to wash your hands.

How to Measure

Metric and imperial measures

We've included two kinds of measurements in this book — metric and imperial. Choose whichever you prefer, but do not switch in the middle of a recipe. Here are the abbreviations we've used:

Metric

mL = milliliter
L = liter
g = gram
kg = kilogram
mm = millimeter
cm = centimeter

Imperial

tsp. = teaspoon
tbsp. = tablespoon
oz. = ounce
lb. = pound

And then there's a pinch and a dash:
A pinch is the amount you can hold between your thumb and forefinger.
A dash is the amount that comes out of a shaker in one shake.

Measuring dry ingredients

To measure dry ingredients, use a measuring cup or spoon the size that is called for. Dip the cup or spoon into the dry ingredient. Then scrape across the top of the cup or spoon with a table knife to level the surface.

Measuring liquid ingredients

Put the measuring cup on a flat surface and pour in the liquid. Check the amount at eye level.

 ## Measuring butter, margarine and shortening

Measurements for butter are sometimes marked on the wrapper. You can also measure soft butter, margarine and shortening as you would dry ingredients.

For hard butter, fill a large measuring cup with 250 mL (1 cup) water. Add the butter until the water rises to the correct amount above 250 mL (1 cup). To figure out how much the water should rise, add 250 mL (1 cup) to the amount of butter you need. For example, 125 mL ($\frac{1}{2}$ cup) of butter will make the water rise to 375 mL (1 $\frac{1}{2}$ cups). Remember to pour the water out before using.

 ## Measuring herbs

When a recipe calls for a herb like thyme or basil, use dried herbs. Fresh herbs are tastier than dried herbs, but you can't always get fresh ones. If you want to substitute, replace 15 mL (1 tbsp.) fresh herbs with 5 mL (1 tsp.) dried, and vice versa.

 ## Sizes

Unless a fruit or vegetable is described as "large" or "small," you can assume you should use a medium-sized one. If the recipe calls for 1 onion and you have only a very large one, use half the large onion.

Helpful Hint

When the ingredient is listed first, measure before cutting. For example, "250 mL (1 cup) strawberries, sliced" means you should measure the whole strawberries, then slice them. But "250 mL (1 cup) sliced strawberries" means you should slice the strawberries, then measure them.

Cookbook Legend

Here are the symbols you'll find at the top of the recipes:

The time it takes to prepare and cook the dish

The number of servings the recipe makes

Recipes suitable for vegans

Many other recipes are suitable for vegans if certain changes are made: use margarine instead of butter, or soy milk instead of milk.

Level of difficulty

These symbols suggest how much experience you need to make the dish:

 Beginner

Easy to make — adult help for younger kids

  Intermediate

Some basic skills needed or some adult help

  Advanced

A bit more complicated or more difficult

Cooking times

We've given you a range of times for cooking most things. For example, "Sauté 2 to 3 minutes" or "Bake 40 to 50 minutes." Check your food after the shortest time. If it's not ready, leave it a bit longer. Electric burners take longer to heat up than gas ones. If you have an electric stove, give the burners a little more time to warm up.

Safety Tips

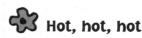

Hot, hot, hot

Use oven mitts or pot holders when touching

▷ pot handles
▷ utensils used to stir or turn cooking food
▷ anything going into the oven or under the broiler
▷ anything that has been on the stove, in the oven or microwave or under the broiler

When you stir a pot, make sure you hold its handle to keep the pot from slipping.

Lifting pots and pans, especially heavy ones, off the stove or out of the oven may be a job for a grown-up. Ask first.

If you are not tall enough to see the bottom of a pot on the stove, you need to wait until you're taller to use the stove.

The steam from boiling water can burn. Be very careful when lifting the lid off a pot of boiling water. Always tip the lid away from you. Also be careful of steam when draining boiling water from a pot. Ask a grown-up to help you drain food in a colander.

Turn, turn, turn

Turn the handles of all pots away from you so that you will not accidentally hit them and spill the contents. Also make sure that the handles aren't over another burner.

Sharp, sharp, sharp

Keep your fingers away from the blades of sharp knives. Always pick knives up by their handles. When using a sharp knife, cut on a cutting board, where the knife won't slip. And cut away from, not toward, yourself.

Blenders and food processors have sharp blades. Keep fingers away from them. Don't forget to turn off or unplug appliances before reaching inside.

Wash, wash, wash

To avoid spreading germs, wash your hands before you start cooking. Make sure your utensils, cutting boards and counters are well scrubbed.

Cleaning up after you're finished cooking isn't fun, but it's part of being a good cook.

Cooking Terms

🔩 Ways of cutting

Slice   To slice a vegetable, hold it firmly against a cutting board and cut down with a sharp knife. Turn your fingertips in so they aren't pointing toward the blade. Always be careful using knives, and watch those fingers!

Dice   First slice, then dice. Hold the slices against the board and cut across the slices, making small square pieces.

Mince   To mince means to cut very fine.

Julienne   To cut a vegetable in julienne style, cut it into long thin sticks.

Grate   Run the cheese or vegetable down the grater until the right amount has collected. Watch your knuckles!

Peel   To peel a fruit or vegetable, take off the outer layer with a small, sharp paring knife or potato peeler.

Core   To core an apple or other fruit, remove the inner part that contains the seeds.

Seed   To seed a cucumber or other vegetable, remove the seeds.

Mincing garlic

To mince a clove of garlic, gently crush it first by pressing on it with the flat side of a knife. Remove the peel. Then cut the clove into slices, turn it and cut across the slices. Continue to chop until the pieces are very small. Instead of mincing garlic with a knife, you can place peeled garlic in a garlic press and close firmly.

Grating gingerroot

To grate gingerroot, carefully cut off the outer coating of the gingerroot and grate the inner part.

 **Ways of mixing**

Stir Stirring is a way of combining ingredients using a spoon or fork.

Beat Beating is very fast stirring. It can be done with a fork, eggbeater, whisk or electric mixer.

Whisk Whisking is a fast back and forth (or side to side) motion with a wire whisk.

Cream To cream two ingredients (usually butter and sugar) mash them together against the bottom or sides of a bowl with a wooden spoon until they are completely combined and smooth. You can also beat them with an electric mixer. It is easier to cream butter, margarine and shortening when they are soft. To soften these ingredients, leave them out of the fridge for a few hours, or put them in the microwave and cook for 1 minute at medium power.

Whip To whip cream or egg whites, stir them very quickly with an electric mixer, eggbeater or whisk. Stirring adds air, and the cream or egg whites will get lighter and fluffier. Stop whipping when peaks form. (If you whip cream too long, it will turn into butter.)

Knead Kneading dough makes it strong and smooth. Place a ball of dough on a counter that has been dusted with flour. Dust a little flour on your hands. Now press the dough down and away with the palms of your hands. Then fold the dough toward you. Turn the dough and push and fold again. Continue until the dough is smooth and soft — usually 5 to 10 minutes.

Chopping onions

To chop an onion, first cut it in half and cut off the ends. Remove the peel. Hold one half against the cutting board with your fingers and slice from top to bottom. Turn the slices carefully and cut crosswise. Onions can be "finely chopped" into small pieces, or "coarsely chopped" into larger pieces.

Chopping canned tomatoes

When a recipe calls for a can of "tomatoes and liquid, chopped," you can either take the tomatoes out of the can, one at a time, and chop them on a chopping board, or you can add the tomatoes and liquid to the pan and then break up the tomatoes with a fork or the end of a spatula.

 **Ways of cooking**

Boil Boiling is heating a liquid until bubbles form and burst on the surface.

Simmer Simmering is just below boiling. Bubbles form on the surface, but only a few break.

Steam Steaming is a way of cooking vegetables in the steam produced by boiling water. Place vegetables in a steamer that sits just above the water. Cover the pot to hold the steam inside.

Fry Fried food is cooked in a frying pan with a little oil or butter until browned.

Stir-fry Stir-fried food is cooked quickly in a little oil in a wok or frying pan and is stirred frequently while cooking.

Sauté Sautéed food is cooked in a little hot oil or butter and stirred frequently.

Bake Food is baked on a rack in a hot oven. Put the pan as close as possible to the middle of the oven. Always use oven mitts when putting food into the oven and taking it out.

Grill Food can be grilled on a barbecue or under a broiler. Wear oven mitts when grilling food.

Broil Food that is broiled is placed under a hot oven broiler for just a short time. Use oven mitts when putting food under a broiler or taking it out.

Melt Foods such as butter or chocolate can be melted in a small saucepan over low heat until they are liquid. They can also be melted in a microwave container in the microwave.

Microwave To microwave food, place it in a microwave container (not metal). Set the microwave for the level and time, and push "Start." Wear oven mitts when removing food from a microwave oven.

✿ Other words

Garnish   A garnish is a piece of food placed on top of a dish for decoration.

Grease   To grease a pan so foods won't stick, put a bit of butter or margarine on a piece of paper towel or waxed paper and rub the bottom and sides of the pan.

Roll   To roll pastry or dough, sprinkle a counter and a rolling pin with a little flour to prevent sticking. Put a ball of dough on the floured surface. Gently press down and away with the rolling pin. Continue back and forth, changing direction each time so that the dough forms a circle. Add more flour if the dough starts to stick to the rolling pin or counter. Stop when the dough is the right thickness.

Marinate   Before they are cooked, ingredients such as vegetables and tofu are sometimes placed in a tasty mixture, called marinade, that flavors them and makes them tender.

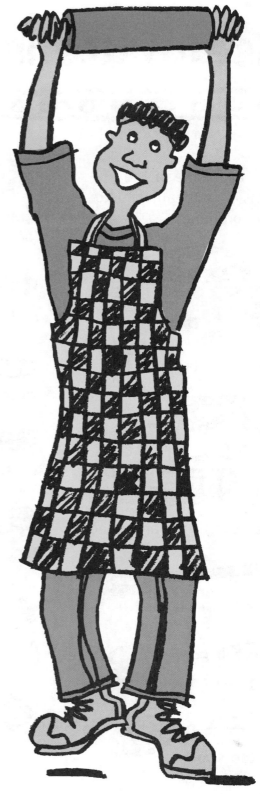

Useful Utensils

Here are some of the utensils you may want to have on hand:

Mixing bowls

Measuring cups and spoons

Wooden spoon

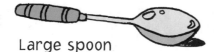

Large spoon

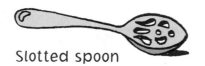

Slotted spoon

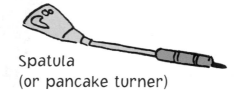

Spatula
(or pancake turner)

Chef's knife

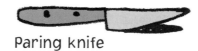

Paring knife

Whisk

Tongs

Potato masher

Eggbeater

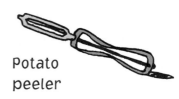

Potato peeler

Garlic press

Skewers

Grater

Juicer

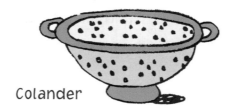

Colander

Sieve

Pastry brush

Muffin pan

Steamer

Rubber scraper

Loaf pan

Wok

Pastry blender

Wire rack

Rolling pin

Cookie sheet

Casserole dish

Cookie cutters

Cake pans

Roasting pan

Breakfast

Hearty Breakfast for a Winter Day
▷ Blender Breakfast (page 251) or Tofu Smoothie (page 252)
▷ Oatmeal Extraordinaire with milk and brown sugar (page 49)

Breakfast for Mother's or Father's Day
▷ Fresh Fruit Salad (page 227)
▷ French Toast or Vegan French Toast (page 30–33)
▷ Tea or coffee

Breakfast in a Hurry
▷ A sliced banana in a bag of Granola (page 26) — Give it a
shake and eat it on the way to school
▷ Juice in a box

Late-Morning Breakfast
▷ Strawberry-Kiwi Smoothie (page 252)
▷ Cinnamon Rolls (page 46)
▷ Hot chocolate
▷ Sliced fruit

Microwave Scrambled Eggs

Level:
Beginner

Makes:
1 serving

Preparation:
5 minutes

Cooking:
2 minutes

Put the bread in the toaster and the eggs in the microwave and you'll have a tasty and healthy breakfast in no time.

You Will Need

2	eggs	2
25 mL	milk	2 tbsp.
2 mL	butter or margarine	1/2 tsp.
	salt and pepper to taste	

Utensils

small microwavable bowl   fork
measuring spoons

1. Crack the eggs into a small microwavable bowl. Beat them with a fork until well blended.

2. Add the milk, butter, salt and pepper. Beat again.

3. Place the bowl in the microwave. Cook on high for 1 minute.

4. Using oven mitts, remove the bowl from microwave. Stir a little.

5. Return to the microwave and cook on high for another 1 minute or until finished.

Try this!

▷ **Cinnamon Toast**
Make a bowl or shaker of cinnamon to sprinkle on buttered toast. Mix 50 mL (1/4 cup) sugar with 10 mL (2 tsp.) cinnamon and keep handy for breakfast or an afternoon snack.

Level:
Beginner
(with help
baking)

Makes:
1.25 L
(5 cups)

Preparation:
10 minutes

Cooking:
30 minutes

Granola

There are lots of breakfast cereals in the stores, but here's one you can make to suit your own tastes. Hate almonds? Try sunflower seeds or cashews. Love honey? Use it instead of the maple syrup.

You Will Need

750 mL	rolled oats	3 cups
250 mL	sliced almonds or other nuts	1 cup
50 mL	brown sugar	1/4 cup
2 mL	cinnamon	1/2 tsp.
2 mL	nutmeg	1/2 tsp.
75 mL	vegetable oil	1/3 cup
75 mL	maple syrup	1/3 cup
5 mL	vanilla	1 tsp.
125 mL	raisins	1/2 cup

Utensils

measuring cup and spoons   wooden spoon
2 bowls, 1 large and 1 small   cookie sheet

1. Heat the oven to 150°C (300°F).

2. In a large bowl, combine the oats, nuts, sugar, cinnamon and nutmeg. Mix well.

3. In a small bowl or large measuring cup, combine the oil, maple syrup and vanilla. Stir.

4. Add the liquid ingredients to the dry ingredients. Stir until the dry ingredients are well coated.

5. Spread the mixture on a cookie sheet. Bake for 30 minutes. Every 5 minutes or so, carefully remove the sheet from the oven using oven mitts and stir the mixture.

6. Let the mixture cool on the cookie sheet. Stir in the raisins. Store in a jar or sealed container.

Serving suggestions

Eat for breakfast with milk, soy milk or yogurt. Grab a handful as a snack. Take a small container of granola to school for lunch along with a small yogurt.

Level:
Beginner

Makes:
1 serving

Preparation:
1 minute

Cooking:
6 minutes
(soft-boiled)
20 minutes
(hard-boiled)

Boiled Eggs

Boiled eggs are a favorite breakfast, but why stop there? Have them for a light supper as well, or take hard-boiled eggs along for lunch or a snack with a little salt and pepper. No packaging necessary!

You Will Need

| 1 or 2 | eggs per person | 1 or 2 |

Utensils

saucepan   tablespoon
knife

Soft-boiled eggs

1. Put the eggs in a saucepan. Add enough cold water to cover them.

2. Bring the water to a boil over high heat.

3. Lower the heat so water is just bubbling. Cook for 4 to 5 minutes.

4. Remove the eggs from the pan with a spoon and run under cold water.

Serving suggestions

Soft-boiled eggs can be scooped out of the shell into a bowl or placed in an egg cup and scooped, spoonful by spoonful, out of the shell. To open an egg in an egg cup, tap the top of the egg with a spoon. With the handle of the spoon, peel away the shell, leaving an opening large enough to fit a teaspoon. If you cut your toast into long, thin pieces (which some people call "fingers" or "soldiers"), you can dip the toast into the yolk.

Hard-boiled eggs

1. Put the eggs in a saucepan. Add enough cold water to cover them.

2. Bring the water to a boil over high heat.

3. Remove the pan from heat. Cover and let stand for 20 minutes.

4. Cool the eggs by running under cold water.

To prevent the eggs from cracking while cooking

▶ Remove eggs from refrigerator and let them come to room temperature.
▶ Before cooking eggs, pierce the large end with a push pin.

To peel a hard-boiled egg

To crack the shell, tap the egg all over on a counter. Hold the egg under cold running water or in a bowl of cold water and gently peel away the shell.

Level:
Intermediate

Makes:
4 servings

Preparation:
10 minutes

Cooking: 10
to 15 minutes

French Toast

It's probably not French and it certainly isn't toasted, but this breakfast treat is a favorite with kids and grown-ups. It's also one of the few dishes that works better with bread that is slightly stale.

You Will Need

3	eggs	3
50 mL	milk	1/4 cup
pinch	salt	pinch
4 slices	bread	4 slices
25 mL	butter or margarine	2 tbsp.

Utensils

shallow bowl (larger than a slice of bread)
measuring cup and spoons   whisk or fork
plate   spatula
nonstick frying pan

1. Crack the eggs into a shallow bowl. Add the milk and salt. Beat until well blended.

2. Dip the bread slices, one at a time, in the egg mixture, first one side then the other. Make sure the egg mixture completely covers the bread and soaks in a little. Set bread aside on a plate.

3. Melt the butter in a nonstick frying pan over medium heat until it bubbles. Turn heat to low.

4. Place the bread, 2 slices at a time, into the frying pan. Let them cook until they are brown on the bottom, then turn them and brown the other side. Add more butter if needed before cooking the next two slices.

Serving suggestions

Most people like their French toast served with maple syrup, but for a change try butter and icing sugar or even jam. Experiment with different kinds of bread, too.

**Level:
Intermediate**

**Makes:
4 slices**

**Preparation:
5 minutes**

**Cooking:
10 minutes**

Vegan French Toast

Just because you don't eat eggs or milk doesn't mean you can't enjoy French toast. You can make the recipe with white bread, but it will be less soggy if it is made with whole wheat or another more solid slice.

You Will Need

125 mL	applesauce	1/2 cup
125 mL	orange juice	1/2 cup
dash	cinnamon or nutmeg	dash
15 mL	margarine	1 tbsp.
4 slices	whole wheat bread	4 slices

Utensils

shallow bowl	spoon
measuring cup and spoons	spatula
whisk or fork	nonstick frying pan

1. In a shallow bowl, combine the applesauce and orange juice. Add a sprinkle of cinnamon. Stir until well blended.

2. Melt a bit of the margarine in a nonstick frying pan over medium-high heat. While the pan is heating, spoon some of the applesauce mixture over one side of the bread. When the pan is hot, place the bread in the pan with the spread side down. Cook for 2 minutes or until golden brown.

3. Spread more applesauce mixture on the top of the bread and turn with a spatula. Cook the other side for 2 minutes or until golden brown. Remove toast from the pan.

Serving suggestions

Serve with maple syrup or jam.

Level:
Advanced

Makes:
1 serving

Preparation:
5 minutes

Cooking:
5 minutes

Cheese Omelet

Our families eat omelets for breakfast, lunch and dinner. Once you have mastered the art of flipping them — which takes a bit of practice — try other fillings as well.

You Will Need

2	eggs	2
10 mL	butter or margarine	2 tsp.
125 mL	grated cheddar cheese	1/2 cup
	salt and pepper	

Utensils

measuring cup and spoons   fork or whisk
grater   small bowl
spatula
omelet pan or small nonstick frying pan

1. Crack the eggs into a small bowl. Beat well.

2. Melt the butter in a frying pan over medium heat until bubbles form and then disappear. Pour the eggs into the pan. Do not stir them, but as they cook, push the edges toward the center so that some egg runs out towards the edges.

3. When the top of the egg begins to look firm, sprinkle with the grated cheese.

4. Here's the tricky part: Slide the spatula under one half of the omelet and lift it over the other half, folding the omelet in half. If some egg runs out, that's fine. If the fold isn't great, don't worry. The omelet will still taste fine.

5. If you like, you can flip the omelet over once more to cook the other side. Then slide the omelet from the pan onto a plate. Season with salt and pepper.

Serving suggestions

Serve with toast for breakfast or lunch, or with potatoes and a salad for dinner.

 **Try this!**

For more adventure, try other fillings: sautéed mushrooms, zucchini and mushroom filling, or sautéed peppers and onion. Other cheeses, or a mixture of cheeses, make a nice change as well. Try mozzarella, blue cheese, Swiss or Emmenthal.

**Level:
Advanced**

**Makes:
4 servings**

**Preparation:
10 minutes
(15 minutes
if cooking
fresh
veggies)**

**Cooking:
15 minutes**

Italian Frittata

A frittata (pronounced fri-TAH-tah) is like an omelet but you don't flip it. Instead the top is cooked by placing it under the broiler. Frittata is the Italian name. In Spain they call this dish a tortilla, which is not the same as a Mexican tortilla, which is a flat bread.

You Will Need

6	eggs	6
75 mL	fresh bread crumbs	1/3 cup
50 mL	milk, tomato juice or water	1/4 cup
15 mL	olive oil	1 tbsp.
15 mL	finely chopped onion	1 tbsp.
1	clove garlic, minced (optional)	1
250 mL	chopped cooked vegetables	1 cup
	salt and pepper to taste	
50 mL	grated Parmesan cheese	1/4 cup

Utensils

small bowl
measuring cup and spoons
whisk or fork
nonstick frying pan with metal handle (not wood or plastic)

spatula
chef's knife

1. Heat the broiler.

2. Crack the eggs into a bowl. Add bread crumbs and milk. Beat until well blended.

3. In a frying pan, heat the olive oil over medium heat. Add the onion and garlic. Sauté for 3 minutes or until the onion is soft but not brown.

4. Add the vegetables. Sauté until the vegetables are heated through. Add salt and pepper.

5. Pour the egg mixture over the vegetables. Stir once. Cook over medium-low heat until the eggs are set.

6. Sprinkle evenly with the cheese.

7. Using oven mitts, place the frying pan under the broiler. Cook for 3 to 5 minutes or until firm and golden.

8. Let the frittata cool for 2 to 3 minutes before removing it from the pan with a spatula. Serve hot or at room temperature.

Serving suggestions

Serve hot for breakfast, or let cool and slice into narrow strips and serve as finger food.

Helpful Hint

If your frying pan has a wooden or plastic handle, wrap it in foil before putting under the broiler.

 Try this!

If there aren't any leftover cooked vegetables in the fridge, such as peas, green beans, chopped spinach, zucchini or broccoli, sauté frozen mixed vegetables for 2 minutes or fresh vegetables for 5 minutes or until tender.

Instead of using Parmesan, try a sharp cheddar or Jarlsberg.

Level:
Intermediate

Makes:
1 serving

Preparation:
5 minutes

Cooking:
5 minutes

Breakfast Burrito

Here's a hearty breakfast with a Mexican flavor. Just the thing to start an action-filled day!

You Will Need

2	eggs	2
15 mL	milk or water	1 tbsp.
	salt and pepper to taste	
15 mL	butter or margarine	1 tbsp.
1	large tortilla	1
25 mL	salsa	2 tbsp.
125 mL	grated cheddar cheese	1/2 cup

Utensils

small bowl	grater
whisk or fork	nonstick frying pan
measuring cup and spoons	spatula

1. Whisk the eggs, milk, salt and pepper together in a small bowl.

2. Melt the butter in a nonstick frying pan over medium heat until bubbles form. Pour the eggs into the pan and cook for 2 to 3 minutes or until eggs look firm, not runny. Turn eggs, or cover the pan with a lid, and cook for another 2 minutes.

3. While the eggs are cooking, heat the tortilla in a microwave on high for 15 seconds.

4. Place the tortilla on a plate and put egg along the center. Top with salsa and grated cheddar cheese. Fold the end of the tortilla up and the sides into the center.

 **Try this!**

For a little more zip, add 25 mL (2 tbsp.) of refried beans (page 224) and a sprinkle of hot sauce.

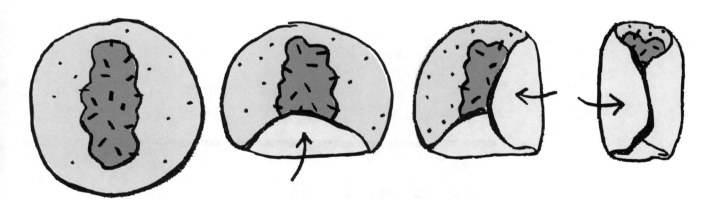

**Level:
Intermediate**

**Makes:
about 12
pancakes**

**Preparation:
10 minutes**

**Cooking:
15 to 20
minutes**

Blueberry Pancakes

Breakfast for the whole family? There's nothing like a pile of pancakes to please everyone.

You Will Need

375 mL	all-purpose flour	1 1/2 cups
50 mL	baking powder	3 tbsp.
15 mL	sugar	1 tbsp.
7 mL	salt	1 1/2 tsp.
1	egg	1
425 mL	milk	1 3/4 cups
25 mL	vegetable oil or butter	2 tbsp.
250 mL	fresh or frozen blueberries	1 cup

Utensils

measuring cup and spoons   whisk
mixing bowl   nonstick frying pan
large spoon   spatula
small bowl

1. Place the flour, baking powder, sugar and salt in a mixing bowl. Stir.

2. Place the egg, milk and oil in small bowl. Beat well with a whisk.

3. Add the egg mixture to the flour mixture. Whisk together until all the lumps are gone. Add the blueberries and stir gently.

4. Heat a little oil or butter over medium heat in a frying pan. With a spoon, pour a little batter into the pan. Repeat until the pan is full of pancakes.

5. When bubbles appear on the top of the pancakes, turn them with a spatula. When the pancakes are brown on the bottom, remove them from the pan.

6. Carefully wipe the pan with paper towels and add a little more oil or butter (not too much) for the next batch.

Serving suggestions

Serve these pancakes hot with butter and maple syrup or icing sugar.

Helpful Hint

If you use frozen blueberries, do not thaw them before you add them to the batter — unless you want blue pancakes!

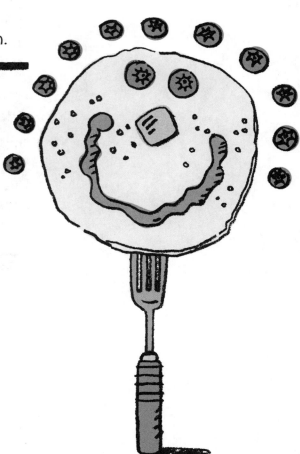

Level:
Intermediate

Makes: 10 to 12 biscuits

Preparation: 20 minutes

Baking: 10 to 15 minutes

Tea Biscuits

Tea biscuits don't have to be eaten with a cup of tea. Break them open and spread them with butter and jam. Then enjoy them with a glass of cold milk for breakfast.

You Will Need

500 mL	all-purpose flour	2 cups
20 mL	baking powder	4 tsp.
2 mL	salt	1/2 tsp.
125 mL	cold shortening or butter	1/2 cup
150 mL	milk	2/3 cup

Utensils

mixing bowl	rolling pin
fork	sharp knife
wooden spoon	cookie sheet
pastry blender	measuring cup and spoons

1. Heat the oven to 220°C (425°F).

2. In a mixing bowl, stir together the flour, baking powder and salt.

3. Add the shortening. With a fork or pastry blender, cut the shortening into small pieces. Rub the mixture with your fingertips until it looks like fine bread crumbs.

4. Add the milk. Stir quickly with a fork until the dough is soft. If it is too dry, add more milk, a tablespoon at a time.

5. Turn the dough out onto a floured surface. With a rolling pin, roll the dough until it is 2.5 cm (1 in.) thick.

6. Cut the dough into squares with a knife. Place the squares on an ungreased cookie sheet. If you prefer round biscuits, use a cookie cutter instead.

7. Bake for 10 to 15 minutes or until just browned.

 **Try this!**

▷ **Golden Tea Biscuits**
Before baking biscuits, brush the tops with a little milk and sprinkle with sugar.

▷ **Raisin or Currant Biscuits**
Add 125 mL (1/2 cup) raisins or currants at the end of step 3.

▷ **Cheese Biscuits**
Add 125 mL (1/2 cup) grated cheese at the end of step 3.

▷ **Buttermilk Biscuits**
Use buttermilk instead of milk. Reduce baking powder to 10 mL (2 tsp.) and add 1 mL (1/4 tsp.) baking soda.

▷ **Sweet Biscuits**
Add 50 mL (1/4 cup) sugar to the flour mixture in step 2.

Level: Intermediate

Makes: 1 large loaf

Preparation: 25 minutes

Baking: 1 hour

Apple Walnut Loaf

Grab a slice of this bread when you need a quick breakfast or snack. It not only tastes good but it's packed with good things like fruit and nuts.

You Will Need

2	eggs	2
250 mL	sugar	1 cup
125 mL	vegetable oil	1/2 cup
250 mL	grated, unpeeled apple	1 cup
5 mL	vanilla	1 tsp.
375 mL	all-purpose flour	1 1/2 cups
5 mL	cinnamon	1 tsp.
2 mL	salt	1/2 tsp.
2 mL	baking soda	1/2 tsp.
2 mL	baking powder	1/2 tsp.
125 mL	coarsely chopped walnuts	1/2 cup

Utensils

large loaf pan
measuring cup and spoons
mixing bowl
wooden spoon

grater
skewer
wire rack
knife

1. Heat the oven to 160°C (325°F). Grease a loaf pan and lightly dust it with flour.

2. In a mixing bowl, combine the eggs and sugar. Stir until light and creamy. Add the oil and beat for 1 minute.

3. Add the apple and vanilla. Stir. Add the flour, cinnamon, salt, baking soda and baking powder. Beat until smooth. Stir in the walnuts.

4. Pour batter into the loaf pan. Bake for 1 hour or until a skewer inserted in the center comes out clean. Cool in the pan for 5 minutes, then transfer to a wire rack to cool.

 **Try this!**

Make two small loaves instead of one large one. Bake for 45 minutes.

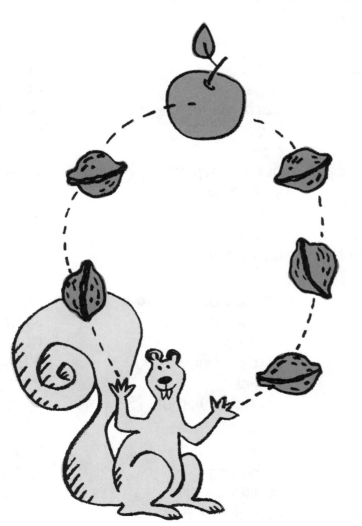

To grate an apple

Wash and dry the apple. Holding the apple by the top and bottom, press it down the side of the grater. Continue until you reach the core. Turn the apple and repeat on the other sides. It is not necessary to peel the apple first.

Level:
Advanced

**Makes: 12
large rolls**

**Preparation:
1 hour**

**Rising:
3 hours**

**Baking:
30 minutes**

Cinnamon Rolls

Make these rolls the night before up to step 12, and let them refrigerate, covered, overnight. The next morning take them out, let them rise and then bake them.

You Will Need

Dough

1 envelope	yeast	1 envelope
5 mL	sugar	1 tsp.
50 mL	warm water	1/4 cup
75 mL	sugar	1/3 cup
2	eggs	2
75 mL	butter, melted	1/3 cup
125 mL	sour cream	1/2 cup
5 mL	vanilla	1 tsp.
2 mL	salt	1/2 tsp.
750 mL–1 L	all-purpose flour	3–4 cups

Filling

250 mL	packed brown sugar	1 cup
10 mL	cinnamon	2 tsp.
5 mL	nutmeg	1 tsp.
50 mL	soft butter	3 tbsp.
125 mL	raisins	1/2 cup
125 mL	chopped walnuts	1/2 cup

Glaze

250 mL	icing sugar	1 cup
1 mL	cinnamon	1/4 tsp.
2 mL	vanilla	1/2 tsp.
15–25 mL	milk or cream	1–2 tbsp.

Utensils

measuring cup and spoons
large mixing bowl
tea towel
wooden spoon or electric mixer
33 cm x 23 cm (13 in. x 9 in.) baking pan

rolling pin
2 small bowls
wire rack
bread knife

1. Place the yeast and 5 mL (1 tsp.) sugar in a mixing bowl. Add the water and stir. Let the mixture stand for 5 to 10 minutes or until it is foamy.

2. Add 75 mL ($\frac{1}{3}$ cup) sugar, eggs, butter, sour cream, vanilla and salt. Mix well. Add about 500 mL (2 cups) of the flour. Mix well.

3. Stir in the remaining flour, 50 mL ($\frac{1}{4}$ cup) at a time, until the dough sticks together but is not dry. You may not need all the flour.

4. Place the dough on a lightly floured surface. Knead for about 5 minutes, or until the dough is smooth.

5. Clean the mixing bowl and wipe it with a little oil. Place the dough in the bowl. Turn it to coat with oil. Cover with plastic wrap or a damp tea towel and place in a warm spot until it is twice the size it was, about 1 $\frac{1}{2}$ hours.

6. With your fist, punch the dough to push out the air. Place the dough back on the floured surface and knead for 1 minute. Cover the dough with the tea towel and let it rest while you prepare the filling.

continued

7. In a small bowl, mix together the brown sugar, cinnamon and nutmeg.

8. Lightly dust the rolling pin with flour and roll the dough into a rectangle about 30 x 60 cm (12 x 24 in.).

9. Spread the butter over the dough. Sprinkle with the sugar mixture, raisins and nuts. Press the nuts and raisins lightly into the dough with a wooden spoon.

10. Starting at a narrow end, roll the dough as tightly as you can toward the other end. Pinch the seam to seal it.

11. Cut the roll crosswise into 12 equal pieces. Grease the baking pan well with butter or margarine. Place the pieces, cut side down, in the pan. Cover tightly with plastic wrap.

12. Place in a warm spot and let rise until twice the size, about 1 1/2 hours. (Or place in the refrigerator overnight. Remove in the morning and let warm for about 30 minutes before baking.)

13. Heat oven to 190°C (375°F). Bake the rolls for 30 minutes or until golden brown.

14. To make the glaze, mix the icing sugar and cinnamon in a small bowl. Add vanilla. Stir in enough milk or cream to make a runny paste.

15. Place waxed paper under a wire rack. Wearing oven mitts, turn the rolls carefully out onto the rack. Drizzle the tops with glaze.

Oatmeal Extraordinaire

Level:
Beginner

Makes:
2 servings

Preparation:
5 minutes

Cooking:
5 minutes

Tired of plain oatmeal? Here's something different.

You Will Need

375 mL	water	1 ½ cups
150 mL	rolled oats	⅔ cup
125 mL	raisins or chopped dried apricots	½ cup
25 mL	maple syrup or brown sugar	2 tbsp.

Utensils

medium saucepan   wooden spoon
measuring cup and spoons

1. In a saucepan, bring the water to a boil. Gradually stir in the oats. Reduce heat and simmer for 3 minutes.

2. Remove the saucepan from the heat. Stir in the raisins and maple syrup. Cover and let stand for a few minutes.

Serving suggestion

Serve with milk, rice milk or soy milk.

Sandwiches, Wraps and Snacks

Vegan School Lunch

▷ Scrambled Tofu Sandwich (page 56)
▷ Carrot sticks
▷ Maple Oat Cookies (page 234)

Summer Lunch

▷ Gazpacho (page 84)
▷ Tropical Cole Slaw (page 108)
▷ Peach-Banana Sorbet (page 228)
▷ Lemonade

After-School Snack

▷ Hummus (page 68) and pita
▷ Sour Cream and Onion Dip (page 70) with veggie sticks
▷ Lemon Poppy Seed Muffins (page 78)
▷ Milk

Basic Sandwiches

Helpful Hint

In a sandwich, use red or Spanish onions. Their taste is sweeter and not as strong as other kinds of onions.

Sandwiches can go with you to school, on a picnic or just out for a walk. All you need is a filling and some bread to hold it together. Experiment and find the combinations for you, whether it's peanut butter and pickles on rye bread or avocado on a pita.

To get you started with your experiments, let's look at the parts:

Bread

▷ Standard loaves: white, whole wheat, sourdough, oatmeal, rye, pumpernickel
▷ Buns, rolls and bagels
▷ Sticks: French or Italian
▷ Flat breads: pita, tortillas, chapatis

Spreads

butter, mayonnaise, tofu mayonnaise (page 214), mustard, horseradish, ketchup

Filling

▷ Scrambled tofu (page 56), store-bought imitation pastrami or bologna (usually made with soy products)
▷ Beans: choose from any of the bean salads in this book; Hummus (page 68); chickpeas fried with some spices, onion and garlic; Refried Beans (page 224)

▷ Cheese: cheddar, processed, Swiss, cream, feta, havarti, brie, camembert, gorgonzola, gouda, goat cheese (chèvre), mozzarella, ricotta, Parmesan
▷ Peanut butter or other nut butters
▷ Vegetables: cucumber, tomatoes, avocado, sweet and hot peppers, onion, zucchini, roasted eggplant or red peppers, artichoke hearts

Garnishes

Lettuce, sliced tomato, alfalfa sprouts, pickles, sliced olives, capers, red onion, salt and pepper

Level:
Beginner

Makes:
Enough for
2 sandwiches

Preparation:
5 minutes

Egg Salad

You can slice hard-boiled eggs on bread for an eggy sandwich, or add a bit extra and make a delicious egg salad. Slip in a bit of lettuce, a slice of tomato or some sprouts for crunch.

You Will Need

2	Hard-Boiled Eggs (page 29)	2
1	green onion, chopped	1
25 mL	mayonnaise	2 tbsp.
	salt and pepper to taste	

Utensils

chef's knife	fork
egg slicer	measuring spoons
small bowl	

1. Peel the shells from the eggs.

2. Place eggs, one at a time, in an egg slicer. Slice, then turn egg and slice across the first cut. (You can also use a knife to slice the eggs.)

3. Place the egg in a small bowl. If you prefer your egg salad smoother, mash the egg a bit with a fork.

4. Add green onion, mayonnaise, salt and pepper. Mix together until well blended.

Deviled Eggs

Level:
Beginner

Makes:
8 half eggs

Preparation:
10 minutes

These are devilishly good at a picnic or as a snack.

You Will Need

4	Hard-Boiled Eggs (page 29)	4
15 mL	mayonnaise	1 tbsp.
1 mL	mustard (optional)	1/4 tsp.
1 mL	lemon juice (optional)	1/4 tsp.
	salt and pepper to taste	
	paprika	

Utensils

paring knife	fork
small bowl	measuring spoons
spoon	

1. Peel the shells from the eggs.

2. Slice the eggs in half lengthwise.

3. Spoon out the egg yolks and place them in a small bowl.

4. Mash the yolks with a fork. Add the mayonnaise, mustard, lemon juice, salt and pepper. Stir until smooth.

5. Spoon the yolk mixture back into the hollows in the egg whites. Sprinkle with paprika for color.

 Try this!

Add 5 mL (1 tsp.) grated cheese, minced pickle or minced olive to each egg.

Fancy Stuff

For a fancy look, put the yolk mixture in an icing bag with a large tip. Squeeze the mixture in a swirling motion (like a soft ice cream cone) into the egg whites.

Level:
Intermediate

Makes:
2 sandwiches

Preparation:
15 minutes

Cooking: 10
to 15 minutes

Raw or Grilled Vegetable Sandwiches

This is one of Erica Glossop's favorite lunches. She varies it according to the vegetables in season, the taste preferences of her friends and what she can find in the fridge.

You Will Need

Dressing

1	clove garlic, minced	1
20 mL	mayonnaise	4 tsp.
5 mL	mustard	1 tsp.
dash	vegetarian Worcestershire sauce (optional)	dash
	salt and pepper to taste	

Sandwiches

4 slices	bread	4 slices
4 slices	cucumber (for raw sandwich)	4 slices
4 slices	zucchini (for grilled sandwich)	4 slices
2	mushrooms, sliced (optional)	2
1/2	avocado, sliced	1/2
1/2	sweet green or red pepper, sliced	1/2
50 mL	grated cheese	1/4 cup

Utensils

chef's knife
spoon
small bowl
grater

toaster
frying pan (if grilling)
measuring spoons

 **Try this!**

For a change, wrap the vegetables in a tortilla.

1. Mix the dressing ingredients together in a small bowl.

2. Toast the bread.

For raw vegetable sandwich

3. Place the vegetables on 2 slices of toast.

4. Top with dressing and your favorite cheese. Cover with remaining slices of toast.

5. Heat in the microwave on high for 30 seconds to melt the cheese.

For grilled vegetable sandwich

3. Heat 10 mL (2 tsp.) oil in a frying pan over medium heat. Add all vegetables except the avocado. Sauté for 3 to 5 minutes.

4. Add the avocado and cheese. Reduce heat and cook for 30 seconds more. Remove heat.

5. Spoon on 2 slices of toast. Add dressing. Cover with remaining slices of toast.

Level:
Beginner

Makes:
2 sandwiches

Preparation:
10 minutes

Cooking:
5 minutes

with
margarine

Scrambled Tofu Sandwiches

This tasty and versatile dish can be made the night before. You can just slap it on some bread or toast in the morning and eat it for breakfast or wrap it up for lunch. It will keep in the refrigerator for up to 3 days.

You Will Need

175 g	firm tofu	6 oz.
10 mL	soy sauce	2 tsp.
10 mL	mustard	2 tsp.
5 mL	turmeric	1 tsp.
	freshly ground pepper to taste	
15 mL	butter or margarine	1 tbsp.
3	green onions, sliced	3
4 slices	whole wheat bread	4 slices

Utensils

chef's knife
fork
measuring spoons
mixing bowl

small frying pan with a lid
wooden spoon
toaster

1. In a mixing bowl, combine the tofu, soy sauce, mustard, turmeric and pepper. Mash together well with a fork.

2. In a small frying pan, heat the butter over medium heat until it bubbles. Add the green onions and stir. Reduce heat to low. Sauté for 1 minute.

3. Add the tofu mix. Mix well. Sauté for 3 minutes or until the tofu mixture is well heated.

4. Toast the bread. Spread the tofu mixture on 2 slices and cover with the other slices.

 **Try this!**

Substitute 1 leek for the 3 green onions and sauté for 5 minutes instead of 1 minute. Wash the leek well before chopping it. Or add 50 mL (1/4 cup) chopped roasted red peppers.

**Level:
Intermediate**

**Makes:
6 to 8 tacos**

**Preparation:
20 minutes**

**Cooking: 15
to 20 minutes**

Vegetarian Tacos

These vegetarian tacos fool most meat-eaters into thinking they are made with hamburger. Serve tacos at a party and let your friends make their own. Just be sure you have lots of napkins handy — or eat outside. Tacos can be messy.

You Will Need

Taco sauce

2	tomatoes, chopped	2
1	clove garlic, minced	1
1/2	onion, finely chopped	1/2
50 mL	chopped cilantro or Italian parsley	3 tbsp.

Filling

25 mL	olive oil	2 tbsp.
1	small onion, finely chopped	1
2	cloves garlic, minced	2
250 mL	textured vegetable protein (TVP)	1 cup
250 mL	water	1 cup
15 mL	chili powder	1 tbsp.
5 mL	soy sauce	1 tsp.
	salt and pepper to taste	

Components

6–8	taco shells	6–8
250 mL	shredded lettuce	1 cup
1	onion, sliced	1
1	tomato, chopped	1
125 mL	sour cream	1/2 cup
250 mL	grated cheddar cheese	1 cup

1. To make taco sauce, combine tomatoes, garlic, onion and cilantro in a small bowl. Mix thoroughly. Set aside. (This sauce will keep in the refrigerator for up to a week.)

2. In a frying pan, heat oil over medium heat. Add onion and garlic. Sauté for 5 minutes or until tender.

3. Add TVP and water. Stir. Stir in chili powder, soy sauce, salt and pepper.

4. Simmer for 5 minutes or until thoroughly heated. Using a slotted spoon, place in a bowl for serving.

5. To serve, bring TVP mixture, taco sauce and other components to the table. For each taco, spread a little TVP mixture across the bottom of the taco shell. Add lettuce, onion and tomato. Spoon sauce and sour cream on top. Sprinkle with cheese.

**Level:
Intermediate**

**Makes:
4 servings**

**Preparation:
10 minutes**

**Cooking:
5 minutes**

Chickpea Tortilla Wraps

Chickpeas are so easy to cook with. This recipe comes from Anne Lindsay, the author of many wonderful cookbooks.

You Will Need

10 mL	vegetable oil	2 tsp.
3	green onions (including tops), chopped	3
2	cloves garlic, minced	2
5 mL	dried oregano	1 tsp.
5 mL	chili powder	1 tsp.
250 mL	diced red or green pepper	1 cup
1/2	tomato, chopped	1/2
1 540-mL can	chickpeas, drained and rinsed	1 19-oz. can
25 mL	chopped fresh parsley	2 tbsp.
	salt and pepper to taste	
4	large soft flour tortillas	4

Fillings
diced tomato
plain yogurt or sour cream
chopped fresh cilantro
shredded lettuce

❀ Try this!

Substitute red kidney beans for the chickpeas, and add 125 mL (¹/₂ cup) grated cheddar cheese.

chef's knife
measuring cup and spoons
wooden spoon
frying pan

mixing bowl
food processor
colander

1. In a frying pan, heat the oil over medium heat. Add the green onions, garlic, oregano and chili powder. Sauté for 2 minutes.

2. Add the red pepper and tomato. Sauté for 3 minutes or until the pepper is tender and liquid is evaporated.

3. Remove from heat. Let cool a minute. Spoon the pepper mixture into a food processor. Add the chickpeas. Process until smooth.

4. Transfer the mixture to a bowl. Stir in the parsley, salt and pepper until well combined.

5. Spoon the chickpea mixture down the center of the tortillas. Top with diced tomato, a drizzle of yogurt, chopped fresh cilantro and shredded lettuce.

6. Fold one side of the tortilla over the filling, then fold one end in and roll up.

**Level:
Intermediate**

**Makes:
2 servings**

**Preparation:
5 to 10
minutes**

**Cooking:
10 minutes**

Quesadillas

Quesadillas (KAY-sa-DEE-yas) come from Mexico but make a perfect cold-weather treat. Judi's daughter, Emma, thinks of them as flat grilled cheese sandwiches and often makes them for lunch.

You Will Need

25 mL	soft butter	2 tbsp.
4	small flour tortillas	4
5	olives, chopped (optional)	5
1	tomato, seeded and chopped	1
½	ripe avocado, thinly sliced	½
125 mL	shredded Monterey Jack or other cheese	½ cup

Utensils

chef's knife	measuring cup and spoons
spatula	2 plates
grater	heavy or nonstick frying pan

1. Butter one side of all 4 tortillas.

2. Turn 2 tortillas butter side down, one on each plate. Put half the ingredients in the center of each tortilla and spread to approximately 2.5 cm (1 in.) from the edge.

3. Place another tortilla on top of each filled one, this time butter side up.

4. Heat the frying pan over medium heat. When it is hot, slide a quesadilla from the plate to the frying pan.

5. Cook for 1 or 2 minutes or until lightly brown on the bottom. Turn with a spatula and cook for 2 or 3 minutes on the other side or until light brown. Lift quesadilla from pan.

6. Remove the pan from the heat to cool briefly. Cook other quesadilla the same way.

Serving suggestion

Cut into quarters and serve immediately with a dollop of sour cream or salsa.

 **Try this!**

The possibilities are endless. Try a variety of cheese and fillings: chopped green onion, peppers or olives; sautéed onions, mushrooms or zucchini; scrambled egg or tofu, whatever strikes your fancy.

Level:
Intermediate

Makes:
6 slices

Preparation:
25 minutes

Broiling:
5 minutes

Bruschetta

Bruschetta (broo-SKET-ta) is often served in Italy at the start of a meal. Try it for an afternoon snack or for lunch with soup.

You Will Need

4	firm, ripe tomatoes, chopped	4
125 mL	chopped fresh basil	1/2 cup
3	cloves garlic, minced or pressed	3
25 mL	olive oil	2 tbsp.
1 loaf	French or Italian bread	1 loaf

Utensils

measuring cup and spoons
chef's knife
garlic press
2 small bowls
spoon

bread knife
cookie sheet
tongs or spatula
pastry brush

1. Heat the broiler.

2. In a small bowl, combine the tomatoes, basil and 2 of the garlic cloves. Mix together.

3. In another small bowl, combine the rest of the garlic with the oil.

4. Cut bread diagonally into 1-cm (½-in.) slices. Place on a cookie sheet.

5. Wearing oven mitts, place the bread under the broiler and toast for 1 to 2 minutes. Carefully turn the bread over with tongs or a spatula and toast the other side for 1 to 2 minutes.

6. Lift the bread off the cookie sheet. Brush each slice lightly with the olive oil and garlic. Spread the tomato mixture on top and serve immediately.

Helpful Hint

If the tomatoes are too juicy, chop them and place them in a colander to drain off some of the liquid before adding the garlic.

Try this!

Drizzle 2 mL (¼ tsp.) olive oil and a squeeze of lemon juice on each slice. Sprinkle with grated Parmesan cheese.

**Level:
Advanced**

**Makes: 16
spring rolls**

**Preparation:
30 minutes**

**Cooking:
20 minutes**

**with
margarine**

Spring Rolls

Most spring rolls are deep fried. Because these ones bake in the oven, they are safer to make.

You Will Need

25 mL	soy sauce	2 tbsp.
25 mL	vinegar	2 tbsp.
25 mL	vegetable oil	2 tbsp.
10 mL	grated gingerroot	2 tsp.
2	cloves garlic, grated	2
500 mL	bean sprouts or finely shredded cabbage	2 cups
2	stalks celery, finely chopped	2
2	carrots, grated	2
1/2	red onion, finely chopped	1/2
1/4	sweet red pepper, chopped	1/4
4 sheets	phyllo pastry	4 sheets
25 mL	butter or margarine, melted	2 tbsp.

Utensils

measuring cup and spoons	wooden spoon
chef's knife	tea towel
grater	pastry brush
large bowl	scissors
fork or small whisk	cookie sheet
small bowl	plastic wrap

1. Heat the oven to 190°C (375°F). Lightly grease a cookie sheet.

2. In a small bowl, combine the soy sauce, vinegar, oil, ginger and garlic. Mix well. Set aside.

3. In a large bowl, combine the bean sprouts, celery, carrots, onion and red pepper.

4. Add the soy mixture. Stir well.

5. Place the sheets of phyllo on the counter. Cover with plastic wrap and a damp tea towel.

6. Remove 2 sheets, keeping the others covered. Brush one sheet with melted butter. Place second sheet on top. Using scissors or a sharp knife cut the sheets into 8 rectangles, by making four evenly spaced cuts crosswise and one lengthwise.

Helpful Hint

To grate the vegetables quickly, place chunks in a food processor and blend quickly.

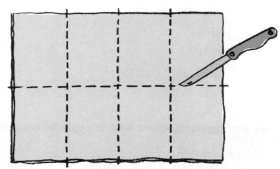

7. Spoon about 50 mL (¹/₄ cup) of the vegetable filling in each rectangle. Fold up one corner. Fold side corners in. Roll up. Place the rolls on the cookie sheet.

Serving suggestions

Serve with Peanut Sauce (page 215) or this dipping sauce:

▷ **Sweet and Sour Sauce**
In a small bowl, combine 25 mL (2 tbsp.) soy sauce, 15 mL (1 tbsp.) rice vinegar, 1 mL (1/4 tsp.) grated gingerroot, 1 grated garlic clove and a pinch of sugar. Mix well.

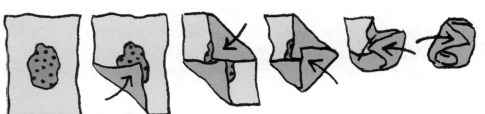

8. Repeat steps 6 and 7 with the remaining sheets of phyllo.

9. Bake for 15 to 20 minutes or until golden brown. Let cool slightly before eating.

**Level:
Beginner**

**Makes:
500 mL
(2 cups)**

**Preparation:
20 minutes**

Hummus

We eat this Middle Eastern treat (pronounced HUM-us or HOO-mus) for lunch and snacks. If you like things hot, add extra spices or sprinkle some hot pepper sauce on the hummus before serving.

You Will Need

1 540-mL can	chickpeas, drained and rinsed	1 19-oz. can
2	cloves garlic, chopped	2
50 mL	lemon juice	¼ cup
50 mL	water	¼ cup
50 mL	tahini	¼ cup
5 mL	ground cumin	1 tsp.
2 mL	hot sauce or cayenne pepper	½ tsp.

Utensils

chef's knife	food processor or blender
juicer	serving bowl
colander	measuring cup and spoons

1. In a food processor, combine the chickpeas, garlic, lemon juice, water, tahini, cumin and hot pepper sauce. Process for 2 minutes or until well blended. If the mixture is too thick, add water 15 mL (1 tbsp.) at a time. Spoon the mixture into a serving bowl.

Serving suggestions

Serve with pita bread cut into wedges. Spread on any kind of bread or wrap as part of a sandwich. Or serve as a dip for cut-up vegetables.

What's tahini?

Tahini is a sesame seed paste that adds extra thickness and yummy taste to hummus. If you like sesame seeds, you will probably like tahini. You can find tahini in most Middle Eastern shops, health food stores and many large grocery stores (look in the international food aisle).

Guacamole

Like hummus, guacamole (gwak-a-MOH-lay) makes a great snack, spread or dip. It can be made smooth or chunky. This version is a bit chunky, but if you prefer, you can blend it smooth.

You Will Need

1	large, very ripe avocado	1
1/2	tomato, diced	1/2
1/2	small onion, finely chopped	1/2
1	clove garlic, minced	1
1	lime or 1/2 lemon, juice of	1
25 mL	vegetable oil	2 tbsp.
1 mL	salt	1/4 tsp.
dash	pepper	dash

Utensils

spoon
measuring spoons
juicer

chef's knife
fork
mixing bowl

1. Cut the avocado in half, remove the pit and spoon out the flesh into a bowl.

2. Mash the avocado lightly with a fork.

3. Add the tomato and onion. Stir.

4. Add the remaining ingredients. Mix well.

Level:
Beginner

Makes:
250–375 mL
(1–1 1/2 cups)

Preparation:
10 minutes

Helpful Hint

▶ If the tomato is very juicy, drain the chopped pieces before adding them to the mixture.

▶ If you make the guacamole ahead of time, place the avocado pit on top to stop the dip from turning brown.

**Level:
Beginner**

**Makes:
250 mL
(1 cup)**

**Preparation:
5 minutes**

Sour Cream and Onion Dip

Super-simple and delicious with potato chips or raw vegetables.

You Will Need

250 mL	sour cream	1 cup
15 mL	onion soup mix	1 tbsp.

Utensils

small bowl   spoon
measuring spoons

1. Combine ingredients in a small bowl. Stir well.

2. Serve immediately or refrigerate for later. It will keep for as long as the sour cream does (check expiry date on container).

Raw Vegetables for Dipping

▷ Before chopping vegetables for dipping, wash them carefully.

▷ Steam very crunchy vegetables such as broccoli for 1 to 2 minutes first (see page 197). Place them in a bowl of cold water after cooking.

▷ Cut the vegetables into pieces that are slightly longer or larger than bite-sized so that the person doing the dipping has something to hold on to as well as something to bite!

 **Try this!**

Add some chopped green onion, parsley or green olives for a change.

Here are some vegetables we like to put on a dipping platter:

Broccoli: medium-sized florets
Cauliflower: medium-sized florets
Carrots: 8 to 10 cm (3 to 4 in.) sticks
Celery: 8 to 10 cm (3 to 4 in.) sticks
Cucumbers: 8 to 10 cm (3 to 4 in.) sticks
Zucchini: 8 to 10 cm (3 to 4 in.) sticks
Green onions: cut off bottoms and tops
Cherry tomatoes: whole (be careful when you bite into them — they tend to spray!)
Mushrooms: whole if very small, or cut in halves or quarters

**Level:
Intermediate**

**Makes:
250 mL
(1 cup)**

**Preparation:
15 minutes**

**Chilling:
30 minutes**

Salsa

Salsa can be used so many ways — by itself, as a dip, added to omelets or as a side dish. Make lots — it keeps well in the fridge.

You Will Need

2	ripe tomatoes, diced	2
2	cloves garlic, minced	2
1/2	sweet green or red pepper, chopped	1/2
50 mL	grated onion	1/4 cup
50 mL	chopped fresh cilantro or parsley	1/4 cup
10 mL	minced hot pepper (optional)	2 tsp.
25 mL	lime or lemon juice	2 tbsp.
	salt and freshly ground pepper to taste	

Utensils

chef's knife	mixing spoon
grater	measuring cup and spoons
bowl	juicer

1. In a bowl, combine the tomatoes, garlic, green pepper, onion, cilantro and hot pepper.

2. Add the lime juice and mix thoroughly. If the mixture is dry, add a bit of cold water.

3. Season with salt and pepper. Refrigerate for at least 30 minutes to let flavors combine.

Serving suggestions

Serve salsa with tacos, tortilla chips or quesadillas (page 62).

Curried Nuts

Level:
Intermediate

Makes:
1 gift

Preparation:
1 minute

Cooking:
1 to 2
minutes

These nuts make a tasty snack or a great gift for people who like their food spicy.

You Will Need

25 mL	vegetable or olive oil	2 tbsp.
15 mL	curry powder	1 tbsp.
250 mL	almond or pecan halves	1 cup

Utensils

nonstick frying pan   measuring cup and spoons
wooden spoon

1. Heat the oil in a nonstick frying pan over medium heat. Add curry powder and stir for 30 seconds.

2. Add the nuts. Stir until they are coated.

3. Remove from heat.
When cool, place in a jar.

Level:
Intermediate

Makes:
12 muffins

Preparation:
20 minutes

Baking:
20 minutes

Applesauce Muffins

Make a batch of muffins and you'll have breakfast and great snacks for days — if these muffins last that long.

You Will Need

125 mL	soft butter or margarine	1/2 cup
125 mL	brown sugar	1/2 cup
125 mL	white sugar	1/2 cup
2	eggs	2
375 mL	applesauce	1 1/2 cups
500 mL	all-purpose flour	2 cups
250 mL	oatmeal	1 cup
5 mL	baking soda	1 tsp.
2 mL	salt	1/2 tsp.
250 mL	raisins	1 cup

Utensils

2 wooden spoons
measuring cup and spoons
2 mixing bowls

12 paper liners (optional)
12-cup muffin tin
skewer or toothpick

1. Heat the oven to 190°C (375°F). Grease the muffin cups or line them with paper liners.

2. In a mixing bowl, combine the butter, brown sugar and white sugar. Mix together with a wooden spoon until creamy.

3. Add the eggs and applesauce. Mix well.

4. In another bowl, stir together the flour, oatmeal, baking soda and salt.

5. Add the flour mixture to the butter mixture. Stir. Add the raisins and stir again.

6. Spoon the batter into the muffin tin, filling each cup about two-thirds full.

7. Bake for 18 to 20 minutes or until a skewer or toothpick inserted in a muffin comes out clean.

8. Let the muffins cool 5 to 10 minutes before removing them from the tin.

Helpful Hint

If you don't fill all the muffin cups, put a little water in each empty cup.

 Try this!

Instead of oatmeal, add 175 mL (3/4 cup) bran and 50 mL (1/4 cup) molasses.

Level:
Intermediate

Makes:
12 muffins

Preparation:
30 minutes

Baking:
25 minutes

Carrot Bran Muffins

These healthy and hearty breakfast muffins are filled with good things: bran for fiber, carrots and applesauce for vitamins, and wheat germ for protein, iron and vitamins.

You Will Need

375 mL	whole wheat flour	1 1/2 cups
125 mL	wheat germ	1/2 cup
125 mL	bran	1/2 cup
15 mL	cinnamon	1 tbsp.
5 mL	baking soda	1 tsp.
5 mL	baking powder	1 tsp.
5 mL	nutmeg	1 tsp.
2 mL	allspice	1/2 tsp.
2 mL	salt	1/2 tsp.
150 mL	orange juice	2/3 cup
150 mL	honey or maple syrup	2/3 cup
75 mL	vegetable oil	1/3 cup
50 mL	plain yogurt	1/4 cup
375 mL	grated carrots (about 3)	1 1/2 cups
125 mL	raisins (optional)	1/2 cup

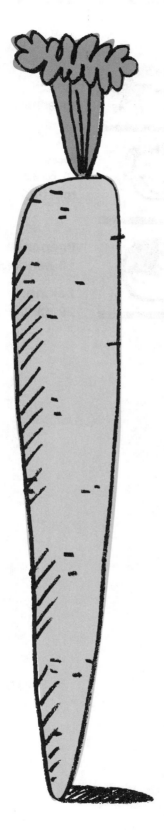

1. Heat the oven to 180°C (350°F). Grease the muffin cups or line them with paper liners.

2. In a mixing bowl, combine the flour, wheat germ, bran, cinnamon, baking soda, baking powder, nutmeg, allspice and salt. Stir.

3. In another bowl, combine the orange juice, honey, oil and yogurt. Stir together well.

4. Add the flour mixture to the wet ingredients. Stir. Add the grated carrots and raisins. Stir until well blended.

5. Spoon the batter into the muffin tin.

6. Bake for 20 to 25 minutes, or until a skewer inserted in the center of a muffin comes out clean.

7. Let the muffins cool 5 to 10 minutes before removing them from the tin.

**Level:
Intermediate**

**Makes:
10 to 12
muffins**

**Preparation:
20 minutes**

**Baking:
20 minutes**

Lemon Poppy Seed Muffins

These muffins are lighter and sweeter than some others. They make a good after-school treat with a glass of milk.

You Will Need

1	lemon	1
250 mL	sugar	1 cup
125 mL	vegetable oil	1/2 cup
150 mL	milk	2/3 cup
2	eggs	2
15 mL	poppy seeds	1 tbsp.
5 mL	vanilla	1 tsp.
500 mL	all-purpose flour	2 cups
15 mL	baking powder	1 tbsp.
5 mL	salt	1 tsp.
125 mL	icing sugar	1/2 cup

Utensils

12-cup muffin tin	2 wooden spoons
grater	small bowl
juicer and a bowl	measuring cup and spoons
chef's knife	skewer or toothpick
2 mixing bowls	wire rack

1. Heat the oven to 180°C (350°F). Grease the muffin cups.

2. Wash and dry the lemon. Grate the rind carefully, removing only the yellow, not the white. Set aside the grated rind. Cut the lemon in half and squeeze the juice. Set the juice aside also.

3. In a mixing bowl, combine the sugar and vegetable oil. Stir with a wooden spoon. Add the milk, eggs, poppy seeds, vanilla and lemon rind. Stir.

4. In another mixing bowl, stir together the flour, baking powder and salt.

5. Add the egg mixture to the flour mixture. Stir until well blended.

6. Spoon the batter into the muffin tin, filling each cup about two-thirds full.

7. Bake for 20 minutes or until a skewer or toothpick inserted in the center comes out clean.

8. In a small bowl, mix the reserved lemon juice and icing sugar.

9. Remove the loaf pan from the oven. Pour the lemon glaze evenly over the muffins. Let muffins cool in the pan, then transfer to a wire rack to cool completely.

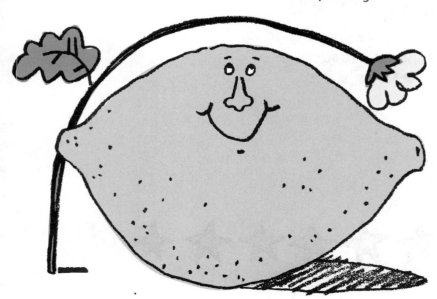

Soups

Quick Lunch

▷ Star Pasta Egg-Drop Soup (page 82)
▷ Quesadillas (page 62)
▷ Orange-Peach Shake (page 251)

Soupy Supper

▷ Minestrone (page 94)
▷ Focaccia (page 183)
▷ Green Salad (page 101)

Curry Lunch

▷ Curried Vegetable Chowder (page 92)
▷ Chapatis (page 190)
▷ Melon slices

Vegetable Stock

Level:
Beginner
(with help straining the stock)

Makes: 1 L
(4 cups)

Preparation:
15 minutes

Cooking:
35 minutes

Vegetable stock is used in many soups and other dishes. You can make your own with this recipe or buy cubes or powdered stock and follow the directions on the package.

You Will Need

2	onions, chopped	2
2	stalks celery, sliced	2
2	carrots, sliced	2
1	peeled or scrubbed potato, cubed	1
50 mL	fresh parsley sprigs	1/4 cup
1	clove garlic, mashed	1
1 L	water	4 cups
5 mL	salt	1 tsp.
8	peppercorns	8

Utensils

large soup pot
chef's knife
measuring cup and spoons

colander or sieve
large bowl

1. Place all the ingredients in a large soup pot. Bring to a boil over high heat. Reduce heat, cover and simmer for 30 minutes.

2. Place a colander over a large bowl. Pour the stock into the colander. Discard the vegetables that remain in the colander.

3. Stock can be stored in the refrigerator for a few days until ready for use, or frozen.

Level:
Beginner

Makes:
4 servings

Preparation:
5 minutes

**Cooking: 10
to 15 minutes**

Star Pasta Egg-Drop Soup

Jennifer's daughter, Erica, adapted this Italian favorite and used to make it for lunch all the time. She taught it to Judi's daughter, Emma, who now continues the tradition. You can use homemade stock or stock made from bouillon cubes or powder.

You Will Need

1 L	vegetable stock	4 cups
75 mL	tiny star pasta	1/3 cup
1	egg	1
2	green onions, chopped (optional)	2
	salt and pepper to taste	

Utensils

chef's knife	wooden spoon
measuring cup	small bowl
saucepan	fork

1. Pour the stock into a saucepan. Bring it to a boil over high heat.

2. Add the pasta. Stir. Bring back to a boil, then reduce heat. Simmer, stirring occasionally, for 5 to 10 minutes or until the pasta is cooked (check the package for cooking time).

3. In a small bowl or measuring cup, beat the egg with a fork until frothy.

4. Bring the soup to a rapid boil. Pour the egg into the soup, stirring constantly with a wooden spoon. Remove from heat immediately.

5. Add the green onions, salt and pepper. Serve topped with chopped fresh parsley. Add a lemon wedge on the side if you like.

 **Try this!**

Along with the pasta, add greens to the soup. Try chopped spinach, kale or bok choy.

**Level:
Intermediate**

**Makes:
6 servings**

**Preparation:
30 minutes**

**Cooling: 2 to
3 hours**

Gazpacho

Gazpacho (pronounced geh-SPOCH-oh) comes from Spain and is perfect on hot summer days: it's refreshingly cold, it tastes great and you don't cook it!

You Will Need

1 796-mL can	tomatoes and liquid, chopped	1 28-oz. can
1	cucumber, peeled, seeded and chopped	1
1	sweet green pepper, chopped	1
1	small onion, chopped	1
1	clove garlic, minced	1
5 mL	salt	1 tsp.
2 mL	paprika	1/2 tsp.
125 mL	water	1/2 cup
75 mL	olive oil	1/2 cup
50 mL	lemon juice	3 tbsp.

Utensils

chef's knife
measuring cup and spoons
mixing bowl
wooden spoon

large glass bowl
blender or food processor
potato peeler
juicer

1. In a mixing bowl, combine the tomatoes and liquid, cucumber, green pepper, onion, garlic, salt and paprika.

2. Put about one-quarter of the mixture in a blender. Process briefly until thick but not smooth. Pour the mixture into a glass bowl. Repeat with the rest of the mixture, one-quarter at a time.

3. Add the water, olive oil and lemon juice to the mixture in the bowl. Stir gently.

4. Chill at least 2 to 3 hours. Stir before serving.

5. Garnish with chopped tomato, green pepper and parsley.

 **Try this!**

If you prefer a soupier soup, add some tomato juice or vegetable juice cocktail.

Serving suggestions

Serve with crusty bread and a salad — a leafy one for a lighter lunch or a bean salad for something more filling.

**Level:
Beginner**

**Makes:
4 small or
2 large
servings**

**Preparation:
5 minutes**

Cold Avocado Soup

This soup is ready in minutes. No cooking, no chilling — just cool, refreshing taste.

You Will Need

1	large avocado	1
125 mL	plain yogurt	1/2 cup
350 mL	milk or cold vegetable stock	1 1/2 cups
	salt and pepper to taste	

Utensils

measuring cup
chef's knife

blender or food processor
rubber scraper

1. Peel avocado and cut into large chunks.

2. Place the chunks in a blender or food processor. Add the yogurt. Blend until creamy. Turn off the machine and scrape down the sides.

3. Add the milk and blend for 15 seconds. Season with salt and pepper. Pour into bowls and serve. Garnish with a spoonful of chopped green onion, tomato salsa or some chopped fresh herbs.

Red Lentil Soup

Level:
Beginner

Makes:
4 servings

Preparation:
10 minutes

Cooking:
30 minutes

Like all beans, lentils provide necessary protein for vegetarians. Unlike some other dried beans, they cook quickly.

You Will Need

15 mL	vegetable or olive oil	1 tbsp.
1	small onion, finely chopped	1
1 L	vegetable stock	4 cups
1 796-mL can	tomatoes and liquid, chopped	1 28-oz. can
250 mL	dried red lentils	1 cup
25 mL	chopped fresh basil	2 tbsp.
5 mL	salt	1 tsp.
	pepper to taste	
dash	hot pepper sauce	dash

Utensils

chef's knife

measuring cup and spoons

large soup pot

wooden spoon

1. In a large soup pot, heat the oil over medium heat. Add the onion. Sauté for 5 to 7 minutes or until golden.

2. Add the stock, tomatoes and liquid, lentils, basil, salt and pepper. Bring to a boil. Reduce heat and simmer for 20 minutes.

3. Add a dash of hot pepper sauce, or more if you like spicy soup. Stir. Serve the soup topped with a dollop of yogurt or sour cream.

Level:
Intermediate

Makes:
6 to 8
servings

Preparation:
15 to 20
minutes

Cooking:
20 to 25
minutes

Potato and Cheese Soup

Here's a soup for a winter's day; the potatoes are filling and filled with nutrition, and the cheese adds protein and zip to the taste.

You Will Need

15 mL	vegetable oil	1 tbsp.
1	small onion, sliced	1
1	clove garlic, minced	1
1 L	peeled and sliced potatoes (4 or 5)	4 cups
750 mL	vegetable stock or water	3 cups
5 mL	salt	1 tsp.
15 mL	chopped fresh parsley	1 tbsp.
500 mL	milk	2 cups
250 mL	grated sharp cheddar cheese	1 cup
2 mL	pepper	1/2 tsp.

Utensils

potato peeler
chef's knife
large soup pot
measuring cup and spoons

mixing bowl
wooden spoon
blender
grater

1. In a large soup pot, heat the oil over medium heat. Add the onion. Sauté for 3 to 5 minutes. Add the garlic. Sauté for 1 minute.

2. Add potatoes, vegetable stock and salt. Bring to a boil. Reduce heat. Simmer for 15 minutes or until the potatoes are tender. Remove from heat.

3. Add parsley and milk. Stir and let cool.

4. Place the mixture a few cups at a time in a blender. Blend until smooth. Place each batch in a mixing bowl after it has been processed.

5. Return the processed mixture to the pot. Add grated cheese and pepper. Stir.

6. Cook over medium heat for 5 minutes or until the cheese is melted and soup is hot. Do not boil. If the mixture is too thick, thin it with additional milk.

Serving suggestions

We serve this delicious soup for lunch with a Caesar Salad (page 107) or Tea Biscuits (page 42), but you could also make it for dinner with an omelet (page 34) or bean salad (pages 116 and 118).

Makes:
4 servings

Preparation:
5 minutes

Cooking:
10 minutes

Miso Soup

Miso soup begins many Japanese meals. Miso is a soybean paste, so this soup is healthy as well as delicious and quick to make.

You Will Need

1 L	vegetable stock or water	4 cups
4	mushrooms, thinly sliced	4
2	green onions, chopped	2
1/4 block	firm tofu, diced	1/4 block
50 mL	miso	1/4 cup

Utensils

measuring cup	small bowl
chef's knife	wooden spoon
saucepan	soup ladle

1. In a saucepan, heat the vegetable stock until just boiling. Add the mushrooms and green onions. Reduce heat and simmer for 1 minute. Add the tofu.

2. Carefully scoop a ladle full of stock from the saucepan into a small bowl. Add the miso and stir until dissolved. Return the mixture to the saucepan. Bring just to a boil. Remove from heat.

❀ Try this!

Replace the mushrooms and green onions with thinly sliced cabbage or carrot. Simmer for 5 minutes instead of 1.

▷ For pesco-vegetarians

For a traditional broth, replace the vegetable stock with 1 L water boiled with 250 mL (1 cup) bonito fish flakes and 15 mL (1 tbsp.) kelp flakes. Strain before making the miso.

Borscht (Beet Soup)

Level:
Intermediate

Makes:
4 servings

Preparation:
10 minutes

Cooking:
30 minutes

Borscht is a bright red soup from Russia. It can be made many different ways with many different vegetables, but it usually contains beets and cabbage.

You Will Need

15 mL	butter or margarine	1 tbsp.
1	small onion, finely chopped	1
250 mL	finely chopped cabbage	1 cup
125 mL	grated carrot	1/2 cup
1 398-mL can	sliced beets	1 14-oz. can
1 L	apple juice or vegetable stock	4 cups
	salt and pepper to taste	
25 mL	lemon juice	2 tbsp.
5 mL	grated horseradish (optional)	1 tsp.

Utensils

measuring cup and spoons chef's knife
grater or food processor large pot
wooden spoon

1. In a large pot, melt the butter over medium-high heat. Add the onion, cabbage and carrots. Sauté for 5 minutes.

2. Drain the beet liquid into a 1-L (4-cup) measuring cup. Add enough apple juice to make 1 L (4 cups). Finely chop the beets.

3. Add this liquid to the pot. Add the beets, salt and pepper. Bring to a boil. Reduce the heat to low and simmer for 15 to 20 minutes or until the vegetables are tender.

4. Add the lemon juice and horseradish.

Serving suggestions

Serve in bowls with a big spoonful of sour cream or plain yogurt on top.

Helpful Hint

If you want to use fresh beets, cook them first without removing the tops, tail or skin. Boil them for 30 minutes to 1 hour (or microwave them, covered, in a little water for 10 minutes) or until they are tender when pierced with a knife. When they are cool enough, hold the beets in cold water. The skins should slide off. Grate or chop the beets before adding to the soup.

**Level:
Intermediate**

**Makes: 4 to
6 servings**

**Preparation:
20 minutes**

**Cooking:
30 minutes**

Curried Vegetable Chowder

This delicious soup not only tastes good, it is so golden it almost glows. You can find canned coconut milk in the international section of most grocery stores.

You Will Need

250 mL	coconut milk	1 cup
25 mL	cornstarch	2 tbsp.
5 mL	salt	1 tsp.
25 mL	vegetable oil	2 tbsp.
1	onion, finely chopped	1
2	carrots, thinly sliced	2
2	stalks celery, thinly sliced	2
2	potatoes, peeled and cut in small cubes	2
10 mL	curry paste or powder	2 tsp.
1 L	vegetable stock or water	4 cups
1	apple, peeled and cubed	1
125 mL	fresh or frozen peas	$\frac{1}{2}$ cup
dash	cayenne	dash

Utensils

small bowl
whisk
large soup pot

chef's knife
measuring cup and spoons
potato peeler

1. In a small bowl, whisk together the coconut milk, cornstarch and salt. Set aside.

2. In large soup pot, heat the vegetable oil over medium heat. Add the onion and sauté for 3 to 5 minutes or until transparent. Add the carrots, celery and potatoes. Sauté for 5 minutes or until the vegetables are tender. If the vegetables begin to stick to the pot, add 125 mL (1/2 cup) water.

3. Stir in the curry paste, vegetable stock and apple. Bring to a boil. Reduce heat and simmer for 20 minutes.

4. Add peas and coconut milk mixture. Increase the heat. Cook, stirring often, until the soup just begins to boil. Season with a dash of cayenne.

Level:
Intermediate

**Makes: 6 to
8 servings**

**Preparation:
40 minutes**

**Cooking:
20 minutes**

Minestrone

This popular Italian soup (pronounced MIN-is-TROH-nee) can be made with other combinations of vegetable or other pasta. Suit yourself and whatever is in the fridge.

You Will Need

25 mL	olive oil	2 tbsp.
1	onion, finely chopped	1
2	large carrots, chopped	2
2	stalks celery, chopped	2
2	cloves garlic, minced	2
1 L	vegetable stock or water	4 cups
1 796-mL can	tomatoes and liquid, chopped	1 28-oz. can
5 mL	dried basil	1 tsp.
5 mL	dried oregano	1 tsp.
2 mL	chili pepper flakes	½ tsp.
1 package	spinach, fresh or frozen	1 package
1	zucchini, chopped	1
250 mL	shell pasta	1 cup
1 540-mL can	romano beans, rinsed and drained	1 19-oz. can
	salt and pepper to taste	
	grated Parmesan cheese	

Utensils

large soup pot
chef's knife
colander

measuring cup and spoons
wooden spoon

1. In a large soup pot, heat the oil over medium-high heat. Add the onion, carrots, celery and garlic. Sauté for 5 minutes or until softened.

2. Add the stock, tomatoes and liquid, basil, oregano, chili pepper flakes, spinach, zucchini and pasta. Bring to a boil. Reduce heat and simmer for 10 minutes.

3. Add the beans. Season with salt and pepper. Simmer for 5 minutes or until the pasta is tender.

4. Serve with lots of Parmesan cheese.

 **Try this!**

Add a spoonful of Pesto (page 218) just before serving.

Level:
Intermediate

Makes:
4 servings

Preparation:
15 minutes

Cooking:
30 minutes

Cuban Black Bean Soup

Beans are an important part of a vegetarian diet, and soups are one of the best ways to eat them. Here's a thick and dark soup to warm you up and fill you up.

You Will Need

Metric	Ingredient	Imperial
2 540-mL cans	black beans, rinsed and drained	2 19-oz. cans
25 mL	olive oil	2 tbsp.
1	onion, finely chopped	1
2	stalks celery, finely chopped	2
1	sweet red or green pepper, finely chopped	1
2	cloves garlic, minced	2
750 mL	vegetable stock	3 cups
1	small bay leaf	1
5 mL	dried oregano	1 tsp.
5 mL	ground cumin	1 tsp.
5 mL	freshly ground black pepper	1 tsp.
15 mL	balsamic vinegar or lime juice	1 tbsp.
dash	hot pepper sauce (optional)	dash
2 mL	salt	½ tsp.

Utensils	
colander	wooden spoon
fork	mixing bowl
chef's knife	measuring cup and spoons
large soup pot	

 **Try this!**

For a spicy soup, add more hot sauce or some cayenne pepper. Start with 1 mL (¹/₄ tsp.), taste and add more if you want.

1. Place half the beans in a bowl and mash them with a fork until they are well crushed. Set aside.

2. In a large soup pot, heat the oil over medium heat. Add the onion, celery, sweet pepper and garlic. Sauté for 10 minutes.

3. Add the vegetable stock, bay leaf, oregano, cumin and black pepper. Bring to a boil. Reduce heat and simmer for 10 minutes or until vegetables are tender.

4. Add all the beans, vinegar, hot pepper sauce and salt. Simmer for 10 minutes. Remove the bay leaf.

Serving suggestions

Serve with a dollop of sour cream on top of the soup and with crusty bread or Cornmeal Muffins (page 187) on the side.

Level:
Beginner
(with help
blending at
the end)

Makes: 4 to
6 servings

Preparation:
15 minutes

Cooking:
30 minutes

Creamy Tomato Soup

This creamy soup contains no milk or cream. The potatoes thicken it and make it a filling meal for lunch or dinner.

You Will Need

25 mL	olive oil	2 tbsp.
1	onion, finely chopped	1
2	stalks celery, chopped	2
1	clove garlic, minced	1
2 mL	paprika	1/2 tsp.
2	potatoes, peeled and cubed	2
750 mL	vegetable stock or water	3 cups
1	small bay leaf	1
	salt and pepper to taste	
1 796-mL can	tomatoes and liquid, chopped	1 28-oz. can
15 mL	lemon juice	1 tbsp.

Utensils

large soup pot
chef's knife
measuring cup and spoons
food processor or blender

potato peeler
juicer
large bowl

1. In a large soup pot, heat the oil over medium heat. Add the onion, celery and garlic. Sauté for 6 to 8 minutes, stirring often. Stir in the paprika.

2. Add the potatoes, vegetable stock, bay leaf and salt. Bring to a boil. Reduce heat, cover and simmer for 15 minutes or until the potatoes are tender.

3. Add the tomatoes and liquid and pepper. Cover and simmer for 10 minutes more. Remove from heat. Remove the bay leaf.

4. Transfer a cup or so of the soup to a blender or food processor. Blend until smooth. Transfer the smooth soup to a bowl. Repeat with the rest of the soup. Return the soup to the pot. Stir in the lemon juice and reheat.

▷ **Herb Croutons**
Cut 4 slices of French or Italian bread into 2.5-cm (1-in.) cubes. Heat 25 mL (2 tbsp.) oil in a nonstick frying pan over medium heat. Add a minced clove of garlic. Stir. Add the bread cubes and 2 mL (1.2 tsp.) dried basil or oregano. Sauté the bread for 3 to 5 minutes or until it browns and gets crusty.

Serving suggestions

Garnish with chopped fresh basil, dill or oregano, or with grated Parmesan or Romano cheese.
Sprinkle some Herb Croutons on top.

Salads

Picnic

▷ Potato Salad (page 112)
▷ Lentil Loaf (page 140) in Oatmeal Bread
(page 192) sandwiches
▷ Deviled Eggs (page 53)
▷ Carrot Cake (page 242)

Greek Meal

▷ Cold Avocado Soup (page 86)
▷ Tomato and Feta Cheese Salad (page 114)
▷ Greek Spinach Pie (page 147)
▷ Baklava

Italian Meal

▷ Bruschetta (page 64)
▷ Caesar Salad (page 107)
▷ Pasta (page 175) with Pesto (page 218)

Basic Salads

Salads offer you a chance to be as creative as you like. You can put everything from marshmallows to pine nuts in your salad. Or you can make a simple salad with just lettuce and a vinaigrette dressing. What's your fancy?

Helpful Hint

In a salad, red or Spanish onions are better since their taste is sweeter and not as strong.

Here are some ideas to get you started:

GREENS

Most salads start with something green. Check out the salad section of your grocery store or supermarket and you'll find
▷ iceberg lettuce — plain, pale and crunchy
▷ Boston lettuce — soft and delicate
▷ leaf lettuce — frilly and bright
▷ romaine lettuce — perfect for a Caesar salad

Then there's arugula, radicchio, endive and even dandelion leaves. And don't forget cabbage for cole slaw and tender young spinach for — what else? — spinach salad.

When faced with a head of lettuce, the first thing to do is remove any tough or brown bits. Tear or cut them off. Then separate the leaves and give them a good rinse in a sink full of cold water. Swish them around to loosen any dirt and rinse them a second time if necessary. There's nothing worse than a gritty salad.

It's important to dry greens well because dressing won't stick to damp greens and will end up at the bottom of the bowl. So spin those greens in a salad spinner, or wrap them in a tea towel and pat them dry. Some people take greens outside and swing the towel around over their head. If you do that, make sure you hold on tight.

After drying, tear (don't cut) the lettuce into bite-sized pieces.

continued

MORE SALAD STUFF

Here are some things you can add to your salad. Remember to wash them first then slice them or chop them into bite-sized pieces.

- ▷ green onions
- ▷ sweet red or green peppers
- ▷ cucumber
- ▷ cabbage
- ▷ celery
- ▷ carrots
- ▷ apple slices
- ▷ cherry tomatoes
- ▷ Spanish or red onion
- ▷ bean sprouts
- ▷ broccoli or cauliflower (you might want to steam them briefly first)
- ▷ mushrooms

To add a bit of protein and make a salad more of a meal, add

- ▷ cheese cubes
- ▷ nuts and seeds: peanuts, pine nuts, walnuts, cashews, sunflower seeds, sesame seeds
- ▷ tofu or soy nuts
- ▷ canned chickpeas or other beans
- ▷ Hard-Boiled Eggs (page 29)
- ▷ cooked pasta (not spaghetti)

Making dressings

One of the easiest ways to make a dressing is to put all the ingredients into a small jar. Screw the lid on tight and shake until everything is well mixed. Shake again just before putting the dressing on the salad. If you have any left over, keep it in the refrigerator with the lid on.

Putting it together

Once your salad ingredients are all in the bowl, put them in the refrigerator until just before you are ready to eat. When it's time, take them out, pour a little dressing on top, give them a toss and serve.

Vinaigrette Dressing

Level:
Beginner

Makes:
250 mL
(1 cup)

Preparation:
5 minutes

This oil and vinegar dressing is a classic and goes with almost any leafy salad. It can be used right away, but the flavor improves if it is allowed to rest for an hour or more in the refrigerator.

You Will Need

1	clove garlic, minced (optional)	1
150 mL	olive oil	2/3 cup
75 mL	good quality vinegar or lemon juice	1/3 cup
1 mL	dry mustard or Dijon mustard	1/4 tsp.
	salt and freshly ground pepper to taste	

Utensils

chef's knife or garlic press   measuring cup and spoons
small jar with a lid

1. Put all the ingredients in a small jar. Put the lid on tight and shake the jar until the dressing is creamy and smooth, about 30 seconds. Refrigerate.

2. Add a little dressing to your salad just before serving.

✿ Try this!

▷ Vary the flavor by adding a pinch of oregano or basil.

▷ Add 5 mL (1 tsp.) dried tarragon, thyme, oregano or basil.

▷ For blue cheese dressing, crumble 25 to 50 mL (2 to 3 tbsp.) blue cheese into the dressing.

**Level:
Beginner**

**Makes:
125 mL
(1/2 cup)**

**Preparation:
5 minutes**

**Chilling:
30 minutes**

Yogurt Dressing

Creamy dressings like this one go well with salads that contain pasta or fruits like apples.

You Will Need

125 mL	plain yogurt	1/2 cup
15 mL	olive oil	1 tbsp.
15 mL	vinegar (fruit, wine or herb)	1 tbsp.
2 mL	sugar	1/2 tsp.
	salt and pepper to taste	

Utensils

jar or small bowl and whisk
measuring cup and spoons

1. Place all the ingredients in a small bowl or jar. Whisk or shake until smooth and creamy.

2. Refrigerate for 30 minutes before serving.

Try this!

Try this dressing with rosemary vinegar on a salad of tomatoes, cucumber, green peppers, red onion and chickpeas. Delicious!

Marinated Cucumbers

Level:
Beginner

Makes:
4 servings

Preparation:
40 minutes
(includes
marinating
time)

Try this instead of pickles at lunch with a sandwich.

You Will Need

50 mL	water	1/4 cup
50 mL	vinegar	1/4 cup
1	cucumber, thinly sliced	1
	salt and pepper to taste	

Utensils

measuring cup   colander
chef's knife   mixing bowl
wooden spoon

1. Put the water, vinegar and cucumber in a bowl. Stir.

2. Cover the bowl and refrigerate for at least 30 minutes.

3. Just before serving, drain the cucumber in a colander.

Level:
Beginner

Makes:
4 servings

Preparation:
15 minutes

Chilling:
45 minutes

Raita

Spicy dishes too hot for you? Serve raita (pronounced RYE-ta) on the side.

You Will Need

1/2	cucumber, peeled, seeded and grated	1/2
250 mL	plain yogurt	1 cup
25 mL	chopped fresh mint (optional)	2 tbsp.
2	green onions, finely chopped	2
1 mL	ground cumin	1/4 tsp.
1 mL	ground coriander	1/4 tsp.
	chili powder (optional)	

Utensils

chef's knife
measuring cup and spoon
large spoon

mixing bowl
grater
potato peeler

1. Place all the ingredients except the chili powder in a bowl. Stir gently.

2. Sprinkle with a little chili powder.

3. Chill 45 minutes before serving.

Caesar Salad

Preparation:
10 to 15
minutes
(longer if
making
croutons)

Traditional Caesar salads include a raw or lightly cooked egg or egg yolk. This recipe uses mayonnaise as a safer alternative.

You Will Need

1	large head romaine lettuce	1
125 mL	grated Parmesan cheese	½ cup
375 mL	croutons	1 ½ cups
Dressing		
50 mL	mayonnaise	¼ cup
1	clove garlic, minced	1
5 mL	vegetarian Worcestershire sauce	1 tsp.
50 mL	lemon juice	3 tbsp.
50 mL	olive oil	¼ cup
	pepper to taste	

Utensils

chef's knife or garlic press measuring cup and spoons
large salad bowl and spoons jar, blender or food processor

1. Break the lettuce into 5-cm (2-in.) pieces, crunchy ribs included, and put it in a large salad bowl.

2. In a jar, blender or food processor, combine all dressing ingredients. Shake or process until well mixed.

3. Pour the dressing on the lettuce and toss. Sprinkle with cheese and top with croutons (page 99).

Level:
Beginner

Makes:
4 to 6
servings

Preparation:
20 minutes

Tropical Cole Slaw

This salad is heartier than regular cole slaw — just the thing for a cold winter night.

You Will Need

1 540-mL can	black beans, drained and rinsed	1 19-oz. can
1 L	finely chopped cabbage	4 cups
250 mL	unsweetened flaked coconut	1 cup
10 mL	sugar	2 tsp.
1	lemon, juice of	1

Dressing

150 mL	olive oil	2/3 cup
50 mL	Dijon mustard	1/4 cup
50 mL	rice vinegar	3 tbsp.
10 mL	sugar	2 tsp.
1	clove garlic, minced	1
2 mL	salt	1/2 tsp.
1 mL	pepper	1/4 tsp.
dash	cayenne pepper	dash

Utensils

measuring cup and spoons
chef's knife
colander
juicer

large mixing bowl
wooden spoon
jar or small bowl and whisk

1. Place cole slaw ingredients in a large mixing bowl. Stir well.

2. Mix the dressing ingredients in a jar or small bowl. Pour over slaw. Toss.

Level:
Intermediate

Makes:
8 to 10
servings

Preparation:
20 to 25
minutes

Cooking:
10 minutes

Pasta Salad with Mixed Vegetables

Make this for a family picnic, or make it for yourself and have lots left over for snacks and school lunches. It will keep in the refrigerator for up to 3 days.

You Will Need

Dressing

150 mL	olive oil	2/3 cup
75 mL	vinegar	1/3 cup
15–25 mL	sugar	1–2 tbsp.
15 mL	lemon juice	1 tbsp.
5 mL	oregano or basil	1 tsp.
dash	garlic powder	dash
	salt and pepper to taste	

Salad

750 mL	tricolor rotini pasta	3 cups
2	large carrots, sliced	2
250 mL	small broccoli florets	1 cup
2	stalks celery, thinly sliced	2
1	small red onion, finely chopped	1
1	sweet red or green pepper or both, finely chopped	1
250 mL	kidney beans, drained and rinsed	1 cup
250 mL	chickpeas, drained and rinsed	1 cup
2	tomatoes, cut into wedges	2

Utensils

steamer and saucepan
large saucepan
measuring cup and spoons
colander

large salad bowl and spoons
chef's knife
jar or small bowl and whisk

1. Mix all the dressing ingredients in a jar or small bowl. Set aside.

2. Bring a saucepan of salted water to a boil. Add the pasta and cook for 8 to 10 minutes or until just tender, stirring so it doesn't stick. (Do not overcook; pasta continues to cook as it cools.) Drain in a colander and rinse under cold water.

3. While the pasta is cooking, place the carrots and broccoli in a steamer over boiling water. Cover and cook for 3 minutes. Drain in a colander and rinse under cold water.

4. Place the steamed vegetables, celery, onion, peppers, beans, chickpeas and pasta in a large salad bowl. Pour dressing over salad and toss together well.

5. Refrigerate for 2 to 3 hours or overnight. Add the tomatoes just before serving.

Level:
Intermediate

Makes:
4 to 6
servings

Preparation:
20 minutes

Cooking:
15 minutes

Potato Salad

This salad is good hot or cold. Make it in the summer to take advantage of fresh herbs.

You Will Need

8–10	small potatoes, cut in 2.5-cm (1-in.) cubes	8–10
125 mL	chopped green onions	1/2 cup
125 mL	tofu mayonnaise (page 214)	1/2 cup
15 mL	chopped fresh mint	1 tbsp.
15 mL	chopped fresh parsley	1 tbsp.
15 mL	chopped fresh chives	1 tbsp.
	salt and pepper to taste	

Utensils

measuring cup and spoons
chef's knife
large saucepan
colander

salad bowl
small bowl
wooden spoon

1. Place the potatoes in a saucepan. Cover with water. Add 10 mL (2 tsp.) salt. Bring to a boil. Reduce heat and simmer for 10 minutes or until just tender. Do not overcook.

2. Drain the potatoes in a colander and place in a salad bowl. Let cool for 15 minutes.

3. In a small bowl, combine the mayonnaise, mint, parsley, chives and salt and pepper. Stir.

4. Spoon the mayonnaise mixture over the potatoes. Toss gently. Serve hot or chill in the fridge and serve cold.

 **Try this!**

Instead of tofu mayonnaise, use 125 mL (½ cup) regular mayonnaise and 10 mL (2 tsp.) Dijon mustard.

Level:
Beginner

Makes:
4 servings

Preparation:
10 minutes

Tomato and Feta Cheese Salad

Fast, easy and delicious.

You Will Need

2–3	tomatoes, cut in chunks	2–3
1/2	red onion, thinly sliced	1/2
12	black olives	12
125 mL	crumbled feta cheese	1/2 cup
25 mL	olive oil	2 tbsp.
15 mL	balsamic vinegar	1 tbsp.
2 mL	dried oregano or basil	1/2 tsp.
	salt and pepper to taste	

Utensils

chef's knife
measuring cup and spoons

salad bowl and spoons
jar or small bowl and whisk

1. Place tomatoes, onion, olives and feta cheese in a salad bowl.

2. Mix the olive oil, balsamic vinegar, oregano, salt and pepper in a small bowl or jar until well blended.

3. Just before serving, toss the salad with the dressing.

Carrot and Raisin Salad

Level:
Intermediate

Makes:
4 servings

Preparation:
15 minutes

with tofu
mayonnaise

When there's no lettuce in the fridge for salad, don't despair. Make this crunchy salad with just a few ingredients you probably have on hand.

You Will Need

4	carrots, peeled and grated	4
125 mL	raisins	1/2 cup
125 mL	peeled, cored and chopped apple	1/2 cup
50 mL	chopped nuts (optional)	1/4 cup
15 mL	lemon juice	1 tbsp.

Dressing

50 mL	mayonnaise	1/4 cup
50 mL	lemon juice or vinegar	1/4 cup
	salt and pepper to taste	

Utensils

chef's knife

measuring cup and spoons

potato peeler

grater (use larger holes)

mixing bowl

small bowl

whisk or fork

wooden spoon

juicer

1. In a mixing bowl, combine carrots, raisins, apple, nuts and lemon juice. Toss together.

2. Put the dressing ingredients in a small bowl. Beat with a whisk or fork until well mixed.

3. Pour over the carrot mixture. Toss well.

**Level:
Advanced**

**Makes:
6 to 8
servings**

**Preparation:
20 minutes**

**Cooking:
5 minutes**

**Chilling:
4 hours**

Four-Bean Salad

This healthy salad provides a good dose of protein and keeps up to 4 days in the refrigerator. The longer you wait, the better it tastes.

You Will Need

375 mL	green beans, cut into 2.5-cm (1-in.) pieces	1 ½ cups
375 mL	yellow beans, cut into 2.5-cm (1-in.) pieces	1 ½ cups
375 mL	canned red kidney beans, drained and rinsed	1 ½ cups
375 mL	canned chickpeas, drained and rinsed	1 ½ cups
1	large red onion, thinly sliced	1
1	sweet green or red pepper, thinly sliced	1

Dressing

150 mL	olive oil	⅔ cup
150 mL	wine or cider vinegar	⅔ cup
15–25 mL	sugar	1–2 tbsp.
5 mL	salt	1 tsp.
	freshly ground pepper to taste	
	chopped fresh basil	

Utensils

chef's knife

measuring cup and spoons

colander

steamer and saucepan

large mixing bowl

jar or small bowl and whisk

spoon

1. Steam green and yellow string beans for 3 to 5 minutes. Let them cool.

2. Combine the kidney beans, chickpeas, steamed beans, onion and pepper in a large mixing bowl.

3. Mix the dressing ingredients in a jar or small bowl.

4. Pour the dressing on the bean mixture. Toss well.

5. Cover the bowl with a lid or plastic wrap and refrigerate at least 4 hours. Toss 3 or 4 times while chilling.

Serving suggestions

Take some bean salad along for lunch or picnics. Or eat it for lunch with sandwich wraps.

Level:
Intermediate

Makes:
4 to 6
servings

Preparation:
30 minutes

Chilling:
1 hour

Black Bean Salad

This easy and delicious salad is a meal in itself. Erica makes this for special occasions, and we all love it.

You Will Need

1 540-mL can	black beans, rinsed and drained	1 19-oz. can
1	stalk celery, chopped	1
1	carrot, chopped	1
1/2	large Spanish or red onion, finely chopped	1/2
1	tomato, diced	1
1	avocado, diced	1

Dressing

50 mL	olive oil	1/4 cup
15 mL	red wine vinegar	1 tbsp.
15 mL	soy sauce	1 tbsp.
1	clove garlic, minced	1
10 mL	lemon juice	2 tsp.
5 mL	dry or Dijon mustard	1 tsp.

1. In a bowl, place the beans, celery, carrot, onion, tomato and avocado. Toss together.

2. Mix the dressing ingredients in a jar or small bowl.

3. Pour the dressing over the salad. Toss.

4. Cover the bowl with a lid or plastic wrap. Refrigerate for at least 1 hour.

Helpful Hint

If you cut up the avocado ahead of time, squirt it with a little lemon juice to keep it from going brown.

**Level:
Intermediate**

**Makes:
4 servings**

**Preparation:
30 minutes**

Tabbouli

A version of this filling salad is found in most Middle Eastern countries. It keeps well in the refrigerator for a couple of days. Bulgur is made from wheat. It cooks quickly and has a nice crunchy texture.

You Will Need

150 mL	bulgur or cracked wheat	2/3 cup
500 mL	water	2 cups
2	ripe tomatoes	2
1	onion, finely chopped	1
250 mL	finely chopped fresh parsley	1 cup
125 mL	finely chopped fresh mint	1/2 cup
1 mL	salt	1/4 tsp.
	freshly ground pepper to taste	
1	lemon	1
50 mL	olive oil	3 tbsp.

Utensils

measuring cup and spoons
saucepan
mixing bowl
sieve

wooden spoon
juicer
chef's knife

1. Put the bulgur in a mixing bowl.

2. Pour the water into a saucepan. Bring to a boil. Pour the boiling water over the bulgur. Let stand for 15 minutes.

3. Drain the bulgur in a sieve. Using the back of a wooden spoon, press out as much water as possible. Return the drained bulgur to the mixing bowl and set aside.

4. Chop the tomatoes into chunks. Place in the sieve and press to remove the juice.

5. Add the tomatoes to the bulgur. Add the onion, parsley, mint, salt and pepper.

6. Squeeze the juice from the lemon. Add the juice to the mixture. Toss. Add the olive oil and toss again.

Serving suggestions

Tabbouli makes a good side salad for hummus and pita or for curries. It can also be added to wraps and Falafels (page 124).

Lunches and Dinners

Spanish Lunch

▷ Vegetarian Tacos (page 58)
▷ Guacamole (page 69) with veggies
▷ Fresh fruit

Weeknight Dinner

▷ Enchiladas (page 158)
▷ Refried Beans (page 224)
▷ Caesar Salad (page 107)

Dinner for Guests

▷ Spring Rolls (page 66)
▷ Thai Stir-Fry (page 132) with
Peanut Sauce (page 215)
▷ Jasmine Rice (page 169)
▷ Banana-Chocolate Delight (page 229)

Sloppy Joes

This meatless version of Sloppy Joes is just as sloppy as the old kind but even easier to make.

Level:
Beginner

Makes:
4 to 6 servings

Preparation:
20 minutes

Cooking:
20 minutes

You Will Need

25 mL	vegetable oil	2 tbsp.
1	onion, finely chopped	1
1	sweet red or green pepper, finely chopped	1
1	clove garlic, minced	1
250 mL	water	1 cup
250 mL	textured vegetable protein (TVP)	1 cup
250 mL	tomato sauce	1 cup
10 mL	chili powder	2 tsp.
	salt and pepper to taste	
4	rolls, buns or English muffins	4

Utensils

heavy frying pan
wooden spoon

measuring cup and spoons
chef's knife

1. Heat the oil in a frying pan over medium heat. Add the onion and sweet pepper. Sauté for 5 minutes or until soft. Add the garlic. Sauté for 1 minute more.

2. Add the water and TVP. Bring to a boil. Reduce the heat and simmer for 3 minutes.

3. Stir in the tomato sauce, chili powder, salt and pepper. Cook over low heat for 5 minutes, stirring occasionally.

4. Cut the rolls in half. Spoon the sauce on the bottom halves. Put the other halves on top.

**Level:
Advanced**

**Makes:
12 to 15 balls
(enough
for 4)**

**Preparation:
25 minutes**

**Cooking:
10 to 15
minutes**

Falafels with Yogurt Sauce

These falafels are pan-fried instead of deep-fried, making them easier — and cleaner — to cook.

You Will Need

1 540-mL can	chickpeas, rinsed and drained	1 19-oz. can
½	red onion, finely chopped	½
2	cloves garlic, finely minced	2
1 slice	bread, torn in pieces	1 slice
2 mL	ground cumin	½ tsp.
2 mL	ground coriander	½ tsp.
2 mL	turmeric	½ tsp.
dash	cayenne pepper	dash
	salt and pepper to taste	
1	egg, beaten	1
125 mL	dry bread crumbs	½ cup
75 mL	vegetable oil	⅓ cup

Utensils

measuring cup and spoons
food processor or blender
colander
chef's knife
whisk or fork

2 cereal bowls
mixing bowl
frying pan
spatula

1. If using a food processor, blend the chickpeas, onion, garlic, bread and spices for 15 seconds. Scrape down the sides and blend for another 15 seconds. OR, if using a blender, blend the chickpeas about 125 mL (½ cup) at a time. You may need to add a little water. Then add the onion, garlic, bread and spices. Blend for 30 seconds. The mixture will be dry.

2. Transfer the mixture to a mixing bowl. With your hands, shape the mixture into walnut-sized balls. Flatten them slightly.

3. Whisk the egg in a cereal bowl. Place the bread crumbs in another cereal bowl. Dip the balls into the egg to coat and then into the bread crumbs. Shake off the excess.

4. In a frying pan, heat the oil over medium heat until it's hot enough to brown a small piece of bread in 30 seconds. Fry the falafels a few at a time for 2 to 3 minutes on one side or until browned. Turn and fry the other side until crisp and browned. Remove them from the pan and drain on paper towels.

Serving suggestions

Serve in a warm pita pocket, garnished with lettuce and tomatoes. Drizzle this wonderful yogurt sauce over the top.

Yogurt Sauce

125 mL	plain yogurt	½ cup
1	clove garlic, minced	1
15 mL	chopped chives, parsley or cilantro	1 tbsp.

1. Whisk everything together in a small bowl until well blended.

Level:
Intermediate

Makes:
4 servings

Preparation:
25 minutes

Cooking:
15 minutes

Vegetarian Burgers

These burgers take a bit longer to prepare than the prepared veggie burgers you can buy frozen, but they also taste a lot better — moist, but nicely crispy on the outside. The recipe comes from UC Berkeley Wellness.

You Will Need

250 mL	water	1 cup
1 mL	salt	1/4 tsp.
125 mL	bulgur, cracked wheat or couscous	1/2 cup
2	large carrots, shredded	2
125 g	firm tofu	4 oz.
1	egg	1
50 mL	chopped fresh mint or parsley	3 tbsp.
50 mL	finely chopped green onions	3 tbsp.
1 mL	cayenne pepper	1/4 tsp.
75 mL	dry bread crumbs	1/3 cup
75 mL	all-purpose flour	1/3 cup
25 mL	ketchup	2 tbsp.
10 mL	mustard	2 tsp.
25 mL	olive oil	2 tbsp.

      Adapted from *UC Berkeley Wellness Letter*, July 2000, page 3.

Utensils

measuring cup and spoons
chef's knife
mixing bowl
saucepan with a lid
grater
sieve

wooden spoon
large nonstick frying pan
nonstick cookie sheet
spatula
fork

1. Put the water and salt in a saucepan. Bring the water to a boil. Add the bulgur and the shredded carrots. Remove from heat. Cover the pan and let stand for 15 minutes or until the bulgur is soft and the water has been absorbed. Drain the mixture in a sieve.

2. Put the tofu in a mixing bowl. Mash it with a fork until it is crumbly. Add the bulgur mixture, egg, mint, green onion and cayenne pepper. Stir well. Add the bread crumbs, 50 mL (¼ cup) of the flour, the ketchup and mustard.

3. Heat the oven to 200°C (400°F). Divide the mixture into 4 equal parts. With your hands, make each part into a patty about 2.5 cm (1 in.) thick.

4. Put the remaining flour on a plate. One by one, place the patties in the flour and turn over to coat both sides.

5. In a large nonstick frying pan, heat the oil over medium heat. Add the patties. Cook for about 4 minutes on each side or until nicely browned and a bit crusty.

6. Using a spatula, transfer the patties to a nonstick cookie sheet. Bake for 5 minutes or until heated through.

Serving suggestions

Serve on burger buns with your favorite toppings: lettuce, tomato, sprouts, ketchup, mayonnaise.

Level:
Intermediate

Makes:
4 servings

Preparation:
10 minutes

Cooking:
20 minutes

Stuffed Portobello Mushrooms

Portobello mushrooms are regular mushrooms grown into giants. They are about the size of burgers and can be eaten, like a burger, in a bun. Because of their texture and flavor, lots of vegetarians call them their version of hamburgers or steak.

You Will Need

50 mL	olive oil	4 tbsp.
1	large onion, thinly sliced	1
3	cloves garlic, minced	3
15 mL	chopped fresh basil or other herb	1 tbsp.
	salt and pepper to taste	
50 mL	water or vegetable stock	1/4 cup
15 mL	soy sauce	1 tbsp.
2 mL	sugar	1/2 tsp.
2	small zucchini, shredded	2
4	Portobello mushrooms	4
125 mL	grated cheddar cheese	1/2 cup

Utensils

measuring cup and spoons
chef's knife
grater
large frying pan

wooden spoon
small spoon
spatula
mixing bowl

1. Heat half of the oil in a frying pan over medium heat. Add the onion. Sauté for 10 minutes or until it is soft and light brown.

2. Add the garlic, basil, salt and pepper. Sauté for 5 minutes.

3. Add the water, soy sauce and sugar. Cook for 3 minutes. Add the zucchini and cook for 5 minutes.

4. Place the mixture in a mixing bowl. Carefully wipe the frying pan with a paper towel.

5. Cut the stems from the mushrooms. With a small spoon scrape away the gills from the underside of the caps.

6. In the frying pan, heat the remaining oil over medium-high heat. Place the mushrooms gills side up in the pan. Cook for 2 minutes. Turn the mushrooms over and cook for another 2 minutes.

7. Turn the mushrooms back gills side up. Spoon the zucchini mixture into each mushroom. Add about 15 mL (1 tbsp.) water to the pan. Reduce the heat, cover and cook for 5 minutes.

8. Spoon the cheese on top of each mushroom. Cover again and cook 2 minutes or until the cheese has just melted.

Serving suggestions

Serve with rice or on a burger bun.

 **Level:
Advanced**

 **Makes:
4 servings**

 **Preparation:
45 minutes**

**Cooking:
15 minutes**

**without
oyster sauce**

Veggie Stir-Fry

Stir-fries are fun and easy once you get the hang of them. Having everything ready to go before you start to cook is a must.

You Will Need

Stir-fry sauce

25 mL	soy sauce	2 tbsp.
15 mL	oyster sauce (optional)	1 tbsp.
15 mL	lemon juice	1 tbsp.
15 mL	sugar	1 tbsp.
5 mL	minced garlic	1 tsp.
5 mL	ground cumin	1 tsp.
2 mL	turmeric	1/2 tsp.

Vegetables

25 mL	vegetable oil	2 tbsp.
1	onion, sliced	1
2–4	cloves garlic, minced	2–4
15 mL	grated gingerroot	1 tbsp.
2	stalks celery, julienned	2
1	carrot, julienned	1
1	zucchini, sliced	1
4	mushrooms, sliced	4
1	sweet red pepper, julienned	1

Utensils

chef's knife
measuring cup and spoons
wok
small mixing bowl

wooden spoon
juicer
grater

1. Mix the sauce ingredients in a small mixing bowl. Set aside.

2. When the vegetables are chopped, put a wok on high heat and add the vegetable oil. It will heat up quickly. Turn the heat down to medium-high.

3. Add the onion, garlic and ginger. Cook for 1 minute, stirring constantly.

4. Add the celery, carrot and zucchini. Stir-fry for 2 more minutes.

5. Add the mushrooms and red pepper. Stir-fry for 2 more minutes.

6. Push the vegetables to the side of the wok and pour the stir-fry sauce in the center.

7. Turn the heat to high. Stir the sauce until it starts to thicken.

8. Stir the vegetables into the sauce. Cook briefly, stirring, until the vegetables are coated and the sauce is thick.

9. Serve over rice.

Helpful Hints

▷ The trick is not to cook all the vegetables the same length of time. Start with the ones that take the longest to cook and work your way down to those that cook fastest.

▷ Any combination of vegetables can be used: broccoli, snow peas, cauliflower. Decide when to add them by how long they take to cook.

▷ If the sauce is not thick enough when you finish, mix 5 mL (1 tsp.) of cornstarch with 5 mL (1 tsp.) of water and stir it into the sauce as it boils. Add a little bit at a time until the sauce is thick enough.

 **Try this!**

Sliced water chestnuts or cashew nuts are delicious additions to any stir-fry. Add them at the end of the cooking.

**Level:
Advanced**

**Makes:
4 servings**

**Preparation:
30 minutes**

**Cooking:
20 minutes**

Thai Stir-Fry

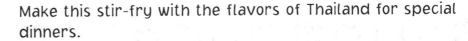

Make this stir-fry with the flavors of Thailand for special dinners.

You Will Need

1	lime	1
50 mL	vegetable oil	3 tbsp.
1	clove garlic, minced	1
5	green onions, thinly sliced	5
1	carrot, cut in thin strips	1
1	sweet red pepper, cut in thin strips	1
1	zucchini, cut in thin strips	1
6	mushrooms, thinly sliced	6
10	snow peas	10
1 227-g can	sliced water chestnuts	1 8-oz. can
10 mL	grated gingerroot	2 tsp.
1 mL	cayenne pepper	1/4 tsp.
	salt to taste	

Utensils

measuring spoons
chef's knife
grater

wooden spoon
juicer
wok or frying pan

1. Grate the rind of the lime. Cut the lime in half and juice it. Set the rind and the juice aside.

2. In a wok or large frying pan, heat the oil over medium heat. Add the garlic and green onions. Sauté for 2 minutes.

3. Add the carrot, red pepper, zucchini, mushrooms and snow peas. Sauté for 2 minutes.

4. Add the lime rind and juice, water chestnuts, ginger, cayenne pepper and salt. Sauté for 5 minutes or until vegetables are cooked, but still crunchy.

Serving suggestions

Serve over rice, rice noodles or chow mein noodles with Peanut Sauce (page 215) on the side.

Level: Advanced

Makes: 6 servings

Preparation: 15 minutes

Cooking: 40 to 50 minutes

Curried Vegetables

Curry, a popular flavor in Asia and the Caribbean, is actually a combination of many spices. Different combinations work better with different foods. Curry paste is available in many stores. If you can't find it, use curry powder.

You Will Need

4	potatoes, peeled and diced	4
4	carrots, diced	4
50 mL	fresh or frozen peas	¼ cup
25 mL	vegetable oil	2 tbsp.
1	large onion, finely chopped	1
2	cloves garlic, chopped	2
25 mL	curry paste	2 tbsp.
1	zucchini, thinly sliced	1
4–6	canned tomatoes, chopped	4–6
15 mL	tomato paste	1 tbsp.
15–25 mL	unsweetened shredded coconut	1–2 tbsp.
	salt to taste	
10 mL	lemon juice	2 tsp.

Utensils

large saucepan
large frying pan or heavy pot with a lid
potato peeler
measuring cup and spoons

juicer
colander
wooden spoon
chef's knife

1. Fill a saucepan with water. Bring to a boil. Add the potatoes, carrots and peas. Reduce heat and simmer for 5 minutes. Drain the vegetables and rinse in cold water. Drain again. Set aside.

2. Heat the oil in a large frying pan over medium heat. Add the onion. Sauté for 4 to 5 minutes or until golden. Add the garlic. Sauté for 30 seconds.

3. Add the curry paste and zucchini. Cook, stirring, for 2 more minutes.

4. Add the tomatoes, tomato paste and some juice from the canned tomatoes to make a thick gravy. Bring to a slow boil. Reduce heat and cover the pan. Simmer for 10 minutes.

5. Stir in the potatoes, carrots, peas, coconut and salt. Cover and simmer for 5 minutes or until vegetables are heated through. Add lemon juice and serve.

Level:
Intermediate

Makes:
4 servings

Preparation:
20 minutes

Marinating:
30 minutes
or more

Cooking:
25 minutes

Baked Tofu

Tofu is made from soybeans, so it's really good for you. By itself it's a bit tasteless — not bad, just bland. It does, however, soak up other flavors. Make this baked tofu when the rest of the family insists on having meat. They may just find they prefer your dinner.

You Will Need

500 g	extra-firm tofu	1 lb.

Marinade

50 mL	soy sauce	1/4 cup
50 mL	vegetable oil	1/4 cup
5 mL	grated gingerroot	1 tsp.
10 mL	sesame seeds	2 tsp.

Sauce

25 mL	peanut butter	2 tbsp.
25 mL	soy sauce	2 tbsp.
15 mL	white wine vinegar	1 tbsp.
5 mL	ketchup or chili sauce	1 tsp.
5 mL	brown sugar	1 tsp.

Utensils

measuring cup and spoons	wooden spoon
grater	shallow nonstick baking pan
chef's knife	spatula
2 bowls	

1. Cut the tofu into 1-cm (¹/₂-in.) cubes and pat dry with paper towels.

2. In a bowl, combine the marinade ingredients. Add the tofu. Stir to coat the tofu. Cover and refrigerate for at least 30 minutes to marinate.

3. Heat the oven to 230°C (450°F). Pour the tofu and marinade into a baking pan. Bake for 10 minutes. Using oven mitts, remove the pan from the oven and turn the tofu with a spatula. Bake for another 5 minutes.

4. While the tofu is baking, combine the sauce ingredients in a small bowl. Remove the tofu from the oven. Pour the sauce over the tofu. Turn the tofu so the sauce coats all sides. Return the tofu to the oven and bake 10 more minutes or until well browned.

5. Let the tofu cool slightly before serving.

Serving suggestions

Serve with rice and a vegetable or salad. Garnish with a bit of chutney, Peanut Sauce (page 215) or even ketchup.

Level:
Intermediate

Makes:
4 servings

Preparation:
30 minutes

Marinating:
1 hour

Cooking:
10 minutes

Tempeh Kabobs

Tempeh is made from fermented soybeans, sometimes with other grains added. Unlike tofu, it shouldn't be eaten uncooked. But like tofu, it soaks up other flavors. Since it has a firm chewy texture, it works well on kabobs and in stews.

You Will Need

1 240-g pkg	tempeh, cut into 2.5-cm (1-in.) cubes	1 8.5-oz. pkg
16	small mushrooms	16
16	cherry tomatoes	16

Marinade

50 mL	vegetable oil	3 tbsp.
50 mL	soy sauce	3 tbsp.
15 mL	grated gingerroot	1 tbsp.
2	cloves garlic, minced	2
1	green onion, finely chopped	1
2 mL	sugar	1/2 tsp.

Utensils

measuring spoons
chef's knife
shallow dish

pastry brush
8 wooden skewers

1. In a shallow dish, combine all the marinade ingredients. Add the tempeh. Stir to coat the tempeh. Let marinate for 1 hour.

2. Meanwhile, soak 8 wooden skewers in cold water for at least 20 minutes so they won't burn.

3. Push a skewer through the center of a piece of tempeh, a mushroom and a tomato. Repeat until only 2.5 cm (1 in.) of the skewer remains uncovered.

4. Repeat with other 7 skewers. Brush marinade over the kabobs.

5. Heat the barbecue. Place the skewers on the grill. Cook for 3 minutes. Wearing oven mitts, turn the kabobs and cook for another 3 minutes or until the mushrooms are cooked and the tomatoes have softened.

 **Try this!**

Substitute other vegetables for the mushrooms and tomatoes. Try pieces of onion, green or red pepper or zucchini.

Serving suggestions

Serve with rice or couscous or wrap in a pita bread.

Level:
Intermediate

Makes:
6 servings

Preparation:
35 minutes

Cooking:
1 hour

Lentil Loaf

Here's a loaf to put in the oven if the rest of the family is roasting something that was once a critter. If you have leftover loaf, slice it for sandwiches or wraps the next day. We like it even better cold, when it is a bit firmer.

You Will Need

250 mL	dried red lentils	1 cup
500 mL	vegetable stock	2 cups
1	bay leaf	1
15 mL	butter or margarine	1 tbsp.
25 mL	dry bread crumbs	2 tbsp.
500 mL	grated cheddar cheese	2 cups
125 mL	finely chopped mushrooms (2 to 3)	1/2 cup
1	leek, finely chopped	1
1	stalk celery, finely chopped	1
375 mL	whole wheat bread crumbs	1 1/2 cups
25 mL	chopped fresh parsley	2 tbsp.
	salt and pepper to taste	
25 mL	lemon juice	2 tbsp.
2	eggs, lightly beaten	2

Utensils

saucepan
measuring cup and spoons
large loaf pan
knife
grater

chef's knife
fork or whisk
large mixing bowl
juicer

1. Put the lentils, stock and bay leaf in a saucepan. Bring to a boil. Cover, reduce heat and simmer for 15 to 20 minutes or until all the liquid is absorbed and the lentils are soft. Remove the bay leaf.

2. Heat the oven to 190°C (375°F). Grease a loaf pan and sprinkle with 25 mL (2 tbsp.) dry bread crumbs.

3. Stir the cheese, mushrooms, leek, celery, whole wheat bread crumbs, parsley, salt and pepper into the lentils. Add the lemon juice and eggs. Mix well.

4. Spoon the mixture into the loaf pan and smooth the top. Bake for 1 hour or until golden brown. Allow to cool for 5 minutes, then loosen around the edge with a knife and turn out onto a serving plate. Garnish with lemon slices and pieces of parsley.

Level:
Intermediate

Makes:
4 to 6
servings

Preparation:
20 minutes

Cooking:
20 minutes

Baking:
25 minutes

Tomato and Cheese Macaroni

When we want something that can be prepared ahead, we make this casserole. It's a bit more work than macaroni and cheese from a box, but worth the effort.

You Will Need

Tomato sauce

25 mL	olive oil	2 tbsp.
1	small onion, finely chopped	1
2	cloves garlic, finely chopped	2
1 796-mL can	tomatoes and liquid, chopped	1 28-oz. can
15 mL	finely chopped fresh basil	1 tbsp.
	salt and pepper to taste	

Macaroni

500 mL	macaroni	2 cups
375 mL	grated Swiss or cheddar cheese	1 ½ cups
250 mL	grated Parmesan cheese	1 cup
50 mL	fresh bread crumbs	¼ cup
15 mL	finely chopped fresh basil	1 tbsp.
15 mL	butter or margarine	1 tbsp.

Utensils

large frying pan   chef's knife
large saucepan   grater
measuring cup and spoons   small bowl
wooden spoon   colander
23 cm (9 in.) square casserole dish

1. Heat the oven to 190°C (375°F).

2. Make the sauce: In a large frying pan, heat the oil over medium heat. Add the onion and garlic. Sauté for 3 to 5 minutes or until the onion is soft. Add the tomatoes and their liquid, basil, salt and pepper. Cook for 10 minutes, stirring occasionally.

3. Meanwhile, cook the macaroni in a large saucepan of salted boiling water for 8 minutes or until just undercooked. Drain well in a colander.

4. Mix both cheeses together in a small bowl.

5. Grease a casserole dish. Spoon a third of the tomato sauce into the dish. Top with a third of the macaroni and then a third of the cheese. Repeat the layers twice. Sprinkle the top with bread crumbs and basil and dot with butter or margarine.

6. Bake for 25 minutes or until the top is golden brown.

**Level:
Intermediate**

**Makes:
4 servings**

**Preparation:
45 minutes**

**Cooking:
30 to 35
minutes**

Lasagna Spinach Roll-Ups

Make these ahead and put them in the oven half an hour before dinnertime.

You Will Need

10–12	lasagna noodles	10–12
1 package	fresh or frozen spinach	1 package
500 g	ricotta or cottage cheese	1 lb.
375 mL	shredded mozzarella cheese	1 1/2 cups
125 mL	grated Parmesan cheese	1/2 cup
2 mL	salt	1/2 tsp.
1 mL	pepper	1/4 tsp.
750 mL	Tomato Sauce (page 216)	3 cups

Utensils

large pot
colander
grater
chef's knife
33 cm x 23 cm (13 in. x 9 in.) baking dish

wooden spoon
large mixing bowl
measuring cup and spoons

1. Heat the oven to 180°C (350°F).

2. Cook the lasagna noodles according to the package instructions until they are tender but firm. Drain. Put them back in the pot and cover with cold water.

3. Thaw frozen or cook fresh spinach. (To thaw spinach quickly, place it in a steamer. Place the steamer in a pot with a little water. Boil, covered, for 5 minutes. To cook fresh spinach, rinse the spinach and place in a pot with the water clinging to the leaves. Cover and cook for a couple of minutes or until the spinach wilts.)

4. Squeeze the water from the spinach and chop it. Place the chopped spinach in a large mixing bowl. Add the ricotta, 250 mL (1 cup) of the mozzarella, the Parmesan, salt and pepper. Mix well.

5. Spread 125 mL (1/2 cup) of the tomato sauce in the bottom of a baking dish.

6. Drain the noodles and dry them on paper towels. Place them on a cutting board. Spread a little of the cheese and spinach mixture on each lasagna noodle — just enough to coat the noodle.

7. Spoon 15 mL (1 tbsp.) of the tomato sauce down the middle of each coated noodle.

8. Roll up the lasagna noodles from the short end and place them seam side down in the baking dish.

9. Spoon the remaining tomato sauce over the rolls. Sprinkle with the remaining mozzarella.

10. Bake for 30 to 35 minutes or until hot and bubbly.

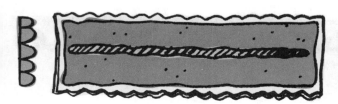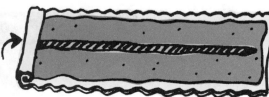

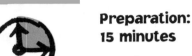

Level:
Intermediate

Makes:
4 to 6 servings

Preparation:
15 minutes

Cooking:
1 hour

Egg Pie

This pie was once known only as quiche. It was very popular because it tasted great and was easy to make. Then someone decided that real men didn't eat quiche, and it lost its appeal. If you call it egg pie, everyone will love it.

You Will Need

1	frozen 23-cm (9-in.) pie shell	1
4	eggs	4
250 mL	table (18%) cream or half-and-half	1 cup
1 mL	nutmeg	1/4 tsp.
1 mL	salt	1/4 tsp.
250 mL	grated or cubed cheddar cheese	1 cup
1 341-mL can	kernel corn, well drained	1 12-oz. can
3	green onions, finely chopped	3

Utensils

mixing bowl
measuring cup and spoons
chef's knife

grater
whisk or fork
baking sheet

1. Heat the oven to 180°C (350°F). Put the pastry shell on a baking sheet.

2. Crack the eggs into a mixing bowl. Beat well. Add the cream, nutmeg and salt. Beat well.

3. Spread the cheese, corn and green onions over the bottom of the pastry shell. Pour in the egg mixture. (Do not overfill the shell or it will spill over the edge while cooking.)

4. Bake the pie for 45 minutes. The filling will puff up and be firm to the touch when it is cooked. Remove from the oven and let cool and settle for about 15 minutes.

Other combinations

Make up your own version. Try sun-dried tomatoes, canned artichoke hearts, sautéed leeks, or other vegetables. For the cheese, what about mozzarella or gruyère, with some Parmesan sprinkled on top? Have fun — just remember not to call it quiche!

Try this!

▷ **Greek Spinach Pie**
To make a Greek version of this pie, substitute 1 package of fresh or frozen spinach for the corn and feta cheese for the cheddar. Thaw frozen spinach and squeeze the water out before adding to the pie shell. For fresh spinach, wash the leaves and steam them in the water that clings to the leaves until they are just wilted. Then squeeze out all the water and chop the spinach before adding to the pie shell.

 Level:
Intermediate

 Makes:
4 servings

 Preparation:
30 minutes

Cooking:
25 minutes

Stuffed Pepper Boats

Sail away on a pepper boat. Peppers aren't the only vegetables that can be stuffed. Try hollowed-out tomatoes or large zucchinis as well.

You Will Need

4	sweet red peppers	4
25 mL	butter, margarine or vegetable oil	2 tbsp.
5	green onions, thinly sliced	5
2	stalks celery, thinly sliced	2
1 341-mL can	kernel corn, drained	1 12-oz. can
6	canned tomatoes, chopped	6
250 mL	grated cheddar cheese	1 cup
125 mL	dry bread crumbs	1/2 cup
	salt and pepper to taste	
125 mL	grated Parmesan cheese	1/2 cup

Utensils

chef's knife
measuring cup and spoons
large frying pan

small baking dish
wooden spoon
grater

1. Heat the oven to 190°C (375°F). Grease the baking dish.

2. Cut around the stem of each pepper and pull out the stem and core. Cut each pepper in half from top to bottom. Remove seeds and "ribs." Rinse well under cold water.

3. In a large frying pan, melt the butter. Add the green onions, celery, corn and tomatoes. Sauté for 3 minutes. Turn off heat.

4. Add the cheddar cheese, bread crumbs, salt and pepper. Stir.

5. Place the pepper halves skin down in the baking dish. Spoon the corn mixture into each half. Sprinkle with Parmesan cheese. Add 75 mL (1/3 cup) of water to the dish. Bake for 25 minutes.

6. Remove peppers from the baking dish and let cool for 5 minutes before serving.

Serving suggestions

Serve for supper with a salad and rice or bread.

Level: Intermediate

Makes: 6 servings

Preparation: 1 hour

Cooking: 45 minutes to 1 hour or more

Chili con Elote

Corn, or elote, a plant native to North America, is common in Mexican cooking. Make this chili in advance and reheat later. Or just leave it to simmer for 2 to 3 hours.

You Will Need

2 540-mL cans	red kidney beans, rinsed and drained	2 19-oz. cans
50 mL	vegetable oil	1/4 cup
1	onion, chopped	1
1	clove garlic, minced	1
2	stalks celery, diced	2
1	sweet green pepper, diced	1
1	carrot, diced	1
250 mL	thinly sliced mushrooms	1 cup
500 mL	vegetable stock	2 cups
1 796-mL can	tomatoes and liquid, chopped	1 28-oz. can
250 mL	corn kernels	1 cup
10 mL	chili powder	2 tsp.
7 mL	salt	1 1/2 tsp.
5 mL	dried oregano	1 tsp.
5 mL	ground cumin	1 tsp.

Utensils

chef's knife
colander
wooden spoon
large pot

small bowl
potato masher or fork
measuring cup and spoons

1. Place half of the beans in a small bowl and mash them with a potato masher or fork. Set both the whole and the mashed beans aside.

2. In a large pot, heat the oil over medium heat. Add the onion and garlic. Sauté for 2 to 3 minutes or until tender.

3. Add the celery, green pepper, carrot and mushrooms. Sauté for 3 to 5 minutes or until tender.

4. Add the stock, tomatoes and their liquid, corn, kidney beans (whole and mashed), chili powder, salt, oregano and cumin. Stir.

5. Cover and simmer for 30 minutes. If at the end of the cooking time the chili is too watery, remove the lid and simmer another 10 minutes.

Level:
Intermediate

Makes:
4 servings

Preparation:
20 minutes

Cooking:
1 hour

African Stew

Peanuts are an important part of many African cuisines. Combined with the sweet potatoes, chickpeas and kale, they give this stew a power punch of nutrients.

You Will Need

1	onion, finely chopped	1
2	cloves garlic, minced	2
1 L	vegetable stock	4 cups
500 mL	diced, peeled sweet potatoes	2 cups
250 mL	chickpeas	1 cup
125 mL	brown rice	1/2 cup
1 mL	salt	1/4 tsp.
50 mL	peanut butter	1/4 cup
500 mL	chopped kale leaves (no stems)	2 cups
25 mL	lemon juice	2 tbsp.
15 mL	soy sauce	1 tbsp.
	hot pepper sauce to taste	

Utensils

measuring cup and spoons
chef's knife
juicer

large saucepan with a lid
wooden spoon
small bowl

1. Heat the oil in a large saucepan over medium heat. Add the onion, garlic and 25 mL (2 tbsp.) of the vegetable stock. Sauté for 3 to 5 minutes or until the onion is soft.

2. Add the remaining stock, sweet potatoes, chickpeas, rice and salt. Bring to a boil. Reduce heat and simmer, covered, for 45 minutes.

3. In a small bowl, combine the peanut butter with 125 mL (1/2 cup) of the liquid from the stew. Stir into a smooth paste.

4. Add the peanut butter mixture and the kale to the stew. Cook for 5 minutes. Stir in the lemon juice, soy sauce and hot pepper sauce.

Serving suggestions

Serve with rice or bread and a salad.

**Makes:
6 servings**

**Preparation:
1 hour**

**Cooking:
1 hour**

Vegetarian Shepherd's Pie

We've fooled many meat-eaters with this vegetarian version of our families' favorite dish.

You Will Need

Potato topping

4	potatoes, peeled	4
10 mL	salt	2 tsp.
50 mL	butter or margarine	4 tbsp.
75 mL	milk	1/3 cup

Filling

500 mL	textured vegetable protein (TVP)	2 cups
500 mL	water	2 cups
25 mL	vegetable oil	2 tbsp.
1	onion, finely chopped	1
250 mL	sliced mushrooms	1 cup
1 340-mL can	kernel corn, drained	1 12-oz. can
250 mL	frozen or fresh peas	1 cup
250 mL	tomato sauce	1 cup
25 mL	chili powder	2 tbsp.
dash	cayenne pepper	dash
5 mL	salt	1 tsp.
2 mL	black pepper	1/2 tsp.
125 mL	grated cheddar cheese	1/2 cup

Utensils

saucepan
kettle or large saucepan
potato peeler
potato masher or electric beater
wooden spoon
measuring cup and spoons
20 to 25 cm (8 to 10 in.) square casserole dish

large bowl
frying pan
spatula
colander
chef's knife

1. Cut the potatoes in quarters and put them in a saucepan. Add enough water to cover them. Add 5 mL (1 tsp.) of the salt.

2. Bring the water to a boil over high heat. Reduce heat and boil for 20 to 30 minutes or until potatoes are done. (To test, stick a fork into a potato. It should go in easily.)

3. While the potatoes are cooking, put the textured vegetable protein in a large bowl. Bring 500 mL (2 cups) water to a boil in a kettle or large saucepan. Pour it over the TVP. Set aside.

4. Heat the oil in a frying pan over medium heat. Add the onion and mushrooms. Sauté for 5 to 7 minutes or until the onion and mushrooms are tender.

5. If necessary, drain the TVP to remove any water. Return it to the bowl.

6. To the TVP, add the onion and mushrooms. Stir well. Add the corn, peas, tomato sauce, chili powder, cayenne pepper, salt and black pepper. Stir again to mix well.

7. Heat the oven to 190°C (375°F).

8. Drain the potatoes and return them to the saucepan.

continued

Helpful Hint

TVP, or textured vegetable protein, is available in most large grocery stores and health food stores either packaged in plastic bags or loose in bulk. It is inexpensive and is very useful in modifying for vegetarians dishes that are usually made with meat.

9. Add 40 mL (3 tbsp.) of the butter, 5 mL (1 tsp.) of the salt and the milk. Mash the potatoes with a potato masher or electric beater until fluffy.

10. Spoon the TVP mixture into a baking dish and press down with a spatula until the mixture is evenly spread over the bottom.

11. Spoon the mashed potatoes onto the meat mixture and smooth into an even layer. Dot the potatoes with the remaining butter. Sprinkle with the grated cheese.

12. Bake for 45 minutes or until the top is crusty and golden brown.

Serving suggestions

Serve with a salad.
If you have leftovers, cover and store them in the refrigerator. They are great reheated the next day.

Chickpea Curry

This Indian curry takes just half an hour to make.

You Will Need

15 mL	vegetable oil	1 tbsp.
1	large onion, finely chopped	1
2	cloves garlic, minced	2
10 mL	grated gingerroot	2 tsp.
1 540-mL can	chickpeas, rinsed and drained	1 19-oz. can
10 mL	curry paste or powder	2 tsp.
1/2 796-mL can	tomatoes and liquid	1/2 28-oz. can
250 mL	water or vegetable stock	1 cup
1/2	lime, juice of	1/2
	salt and pepper to taste	

Utensils

measuring cup and spoons   chef's knife
grater   large frying pan
wooden spoon   colander
juicer

1. Heat the oil in a large frying pan over medium heat. Add the onion, garlic and ginger. Sauté for 5 minutes or until onion is tender.

2. Add the chickpeas. Chop the tomatoes and add them to the pan along with liquid from the can. Simmer, stirring occasionally, for 10 minutes.

3. Add the water, lime juice, salt and pepper. Simmer, stirring occasionally, for 10 minutes.

Serving suggestions

▷ Delicious over basmati rice (page 169), in a roti or with chapatis (page 190).
▷ Chutney, a spicy Indian jam, goes well with curries, as does Raita (page 106).

Level: Intermediate

Makes: 4 to 6 servings

Preparation: 15 to 20 minutes

Cooking: 45 minutes (includes cooling time)

Enchiladas

Here's a Mexican dish that you can serve a million different ways by changing the filling, the sauce or the topping.

You Will Need

50 mL	olive oil	3 tbsp.
1	sweet yellow pepper, cut in 1-cm (½-in.) pieces	1
1	sweet red pepper, cut in 1-cm (½-in.) pieces	1
½	red onion, chopped	½
2	cloves garlic, minced	2
1 540-mL can	black beans, rinsed and drained	1 19-oz. can
1 340-mL can	kernel corn, drained	1 12-oz. can
2	limes, juice of	2
10 mL	dried basil (or 15 mL/1 tbsp. chopped fresh basil)	1 tsp.
	salt and pepper to taste	
250 mL	salsa	1 cup
250 mL	tomato sauce	1 cup
125 mL	water	½ cup
5 or 6	large tortillas	5 or 6

Utensils

colander
juicer
measuring cup and spoons
chef's knife

large frying pan
bowl
wooden spoon

 Try this!

Substitute other vegetables or canned beans for those in the recipe. Try with hot or mild salsa, whichever you prefer. Sprinkle 125 mL (1/2 cup) grated cheese on top before baking. Or put some cheese inside the enchiladas. Use your imagination!

1. In a large frying pan, heat the oil over medium heat. Add the peppers, onion and garlic. Sauté for 5 minutes. Add the beans, corn, lime juice, basil, salt and pepper. Stir. Remove from heat.

2. In a bowl, combine the salsa, tomato sauce and water. Stir well. Spread about 175 mL (3/4 cup) of the mixture over the bottom of a casserole dish.

3. Place about 125 mL (1/2 cup) of the vegetable mixture on one side of a large tortilla. Fold up about one third, then roll.

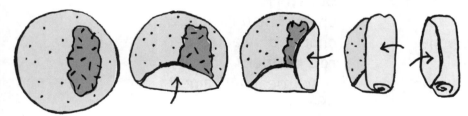

If needed, spoon a bit more mixture in the open end of the roll. Place the roll, seam side down, in the casserole. Repeat with remaining tortillas, placing them side by side in the casserole.

4. Mix the remaining salsa mixture with any remaining vegetable mixture. Spoon on top of the enchiladas. Bake for 30 minutes. Let cool for 10 minutes before serving.

Serving suggestions

Serve with a salad.

Level:
Intermediate

Makes:
4 servings

Preparation:
10 minutes

Cooking:
20 minutes
for white
rice,
40 minutes
for brown
rice

Rice and Beans

When you want to get all your essential proteins in one dish, make Rice and Beans, then add vegetables for even more flavor and nutrition.

You Will Need

500 mL	water	2 cups
5 mL	ground cumin	1 tsp.
5 mL	chili powder	1 tsp.
2 mL	salt	1/2 tsp.
dash	cayenne pepper	dash
250 mL	long-grain white or brown rice	1 cup
1/2	onion, finely chopped	1/2
125 mL	chopped sweet green or red pepper	1/2 cup
1 540-mL can	black beans, drained and rinsed	1 19-oz. can

Optional ingredients

1	green onion, sliced	1
50 mL	cooked peas	1/4 cup
1	small carrot, shredded	1
1	tomato, diced	1
1	avocado, diced	1

Utensils

chef's knife
measuring cup and spoons
grater
saucepan with a lid

fork
wooden spoon
colander

Helpful Hint

Be sure to rinse the beans well — for at least 30 seconds under cold running water.

1. Put the water in a saucepan. Bring to a boil. Add the cumin, chili powder, salt and cayenne pepper. Stir.

2. Add the rice, onion and sweet pepper. Stir.

3. Cover the pan and reduce the heat to the lowest possible setting. Cook for 15 minutes for white rice and 35 minutes for brown rice. Remove from heat and let stand for 5 minutes without removing the lid.

4. Fluff the rice with the fork. Add the beans and any of the optional ingredients that you like. Stir gently with a fork.

without egg

Sushi

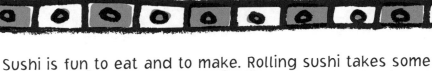

Sushi is fun to eat and to make. Rolling sushi takes some practice, but once you get the hang of it, you can make this special treat whenever you like.

You Will Need

500 mL	Japanese short-grain rice	2 cups
pinch	salt	pinch
500 mL	water	2 cups
50 mL	rice vinegar	1/4 cup
25 mL	sugar	2 tbsp.
1/2	English cucumber, peeled and seeded	1/2
1	avocado	1
1	egg (optional)	1
6 sheets	nori (roasted seaweed)	6 sheets

Utensils

measuring cup and spoons
sieve
saucepan with a lid
wooden spoon
small saucepan
small nonstick frying pan, spatula and small bowl
(for egg, if using)

small non-metallic bowl
chef's knife
potato peeler
bamboo mat (optional)
fork

1. Put the rice in a sieve and rinse it under cold running water.

2. Put the rice and salt in a saucepan with the water. Bring to a boil. Reduce heat. Cover and simmer for 15 minutes.

3. Turn off the heat and leave it covered for another 10 minutes. Then put the rice in a non-metal bowl. Fluff with a fork.

4. In a small saucepan, mix the rice vinegar and sugar. Bring to a boil, stirring.

5. Drizzle the sugar mixture over the rice while fluffing the rice with a fork. Let cool.

6. If using egg, carefully crack the egg into a small bowl. Add a pinch of salt and a pinch of sugar. Beat gently with a fork. Heat 5 mL (1 tsp.) butter in a nonstick frying pan. When it bubbles, pour in egg mixture and tip the pan so it reaches the sides. When bubbles form on the surface of the egg, use a spatula to flip it over. When cooked (after about another 30 seconds), slide the omelet onto a cutting board or plate.

7. Slice the cucumber, avocado and egg in long strips.

continued

To make a sushi hand roll

8. Cut one sheet of nori in half. Heat in a microwave or toaster-oven on high for 10 seconds to soften it.

9. Place the nori shiny side down. Spread a little rice on the left side of the nori. Top with the other ingredients.

10. Starting from the left, roll the nori into a cone. Repeat with remaining nori.

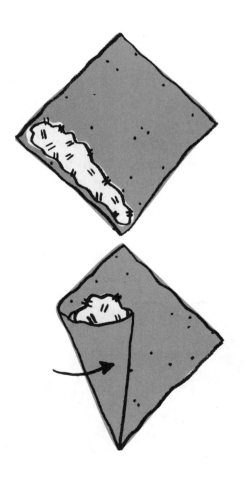

To make a maki-sushi roll

8. Microwave one whole sheet of nori on high for 10 seconds to soften it (or use a toaster-oven).

9. Place the nori on a bamboo mat or a counter. With a fork, spread some rice thinly on the bottom third of the nori. Top with the other ingredients placed in a line.

10. Wet your fingers slightly. Using the bamboo mat or your fingers, roll the nori and the ingredients away from you as tightly as possible without tearing the nori. You may need to wet the outside edge slightly to help it stay closed.

Helpful Hint

Nori, wasabi, bamboo mats and pickled ginger are available in Japanese grocery stores and some health food stores.

 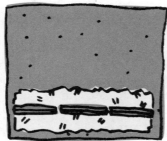 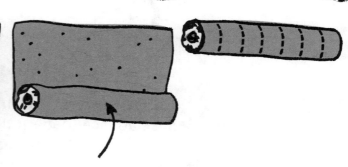

11. Place the roll on a cutting board. With a very sharp knife, slice the roll into 7 or 8 bite-sized pieces. To keep the knife from sticking, run it through a slice of lemon after each cut.

12. Repeat with remaining ingredients.

13. Serve with pickled ginger and with a little soy sauce mixed with some wasabi (Japanese horseradish), if desired.

Rice, Pasta and Noodles

Indian Lunch

▷Dal (page 222) with vegetables added
▷Basmati Rice (page 169) or Chapatis (page 190)
▷Raita (page 106)
▷Sorbet (page 228) with raspberries and banana

Dinner for One

▷Simple Pasta for One (page 176)
▷Spinach salad with Yogurt Dressing (page 104) and walnuts
▷Crusty bread

Saturday-Night Dinner

▷Baked Tofu (page 136)
▷Peanut Sauce (page 215)
▷Risotto (page 172)
▷Green Beans with Almonds (page 199)

Basic Rice

Rice grows on a plant that is partially submerged in water. The grain of rice is actually the seed of the plant.

White rice is the most common rice. The seed's husk, bran and some of the germ have been removed, making it less nutritious but whiter in color and quicker to cook. Brown rice is the whole grain. Only the outer husk has been removed. The most nutritious rice, it has a slightly nutty flavor and is chewier. It also takes longer to cook.

White rice is also treated in other ways:
▷ Enriched rice has had some of the nutrients added back in a coating.
▷ Parboiled, or converted, rice has had the nutrients forced back by steaming it under pressure.
▷ Instant rice is precooked and has the least flavor, but cooks quickly.

You can also find some other kinds of rice:
▷ Fragrant rices have a different taste and a very long grain. The most common are basmati from India, Pakistan and the Middle East, and jasmine from Thailand.

▷ Arborio rice from Italy has a shorter grain and is popular in an Italian dish called risotto (page 172), which is cooked slowly so the rice absorbs the flavor of the cooking liquid.
▷ Sweet rice is a short-grain rice that is stickier than long-grain and is used in Asian cooking.

**Level:
Beginner**

**Makes:
4 servings**

**Preparation:
5 minutes**

**Cooking:
20 minutes
for white
rice
40 minutes
for brown
rice**

Boiled Rice

There are many different ways to cook rice. You can follow the instructions on the package or use this foolproof method for perfect rice every time.

You Will Need

500 mL	water	2 cups
2 mL	salt	½ tsp.
250 mL	long-grain rice	1 cup

Utensils

measuring cup and spoons   saucepan with a lid
fork

Helpful Hint

▷ If all the water is not absorbed at the end of cooking, put the uncovered pot in a 150°C (300°F) oven for a few minutes until the grains separate.

▷ If the rice isn't cooked, sprinkle with water and cook, covered, for another few minutes.

1. Put the water and salt in a saucepan. Bring the water to a boil.

2. Add the rice and stir gently with a fork.

3. Cover and reduce heat to lowest possible setting. Cook for 15 minutes for white rice, 30 minutes for brown. Do not lift the lid.

4. Remove from heat. Let stand, covered, 5 minutes for white, 10 minutes for brown. Remove the lid and fluff the rice with the fork.

Basmati and Jasmine Rice

These Asian rices with their delicate aromas are very popular.

Level: Beginner

Makes: 4 servings

Preparation: 5 minutes

Cooking: 25 minutes

You Will Need

250 mL	basmati or jasmine rice	1 cup
15 mL	vegetable oil	1 tbsp.
1/2	onion, chopped	1/2
500 mL	water	2 cups

Utensils

measuring cup and spoons
chef's knife
sieve

saucepan with a lid
wooden spoon

1. Place the rice in a sieve and rinse under cold water for 1 minute.

2. Heat the oil in a saucepan over medium heat. Add the onion. Sauté for 3 minutes. Add the rice. Sauté for 3 minutes or until the rice is transparent.

3. Add the water. Increase heat to high. When the water boils, cover the pot and reduce the heat as low as possible. Simmer, without lifting the lid, for 15 minutes. Remove from heat and let stand for 5 minutes.

4. Fluff the rice with a fork before serving.

Serving suggestions

Serve topped with curry (pages 134 and 157) or Dal (page 222), or as a side dish for Vegetarian Burgers (page 126) or Lentil Loaf (page 140).

Level:
Intermediate

Makes:
4 servings

Preparation:
5 minutes

Cooking:
30 minutes

Vegetable Pilau

For a slightly fancier rice dish, try this. Frozen mixed vegetables are faster to use. If you are using fresh vegetables, chop them and sauté them in a little oil for 5 minutes first.

You Will Need

25 mL	butter or margarine	2 tbsp.
1	onion, thinly sliced	1
1	bay leaf	1
pinch	ground cumin	pinch
pinch	cinnamon	pinch
250 mL	rice	1 cup
250 mL	frozen mixed vegetables	1 cup
500 mL	water or vegetable stock	2 cups
	salt and pepper to taste	
dash	cayenne pepper	dash

Utensils

chef's knife
measuring cup and spoons
wooden spoon

saucepan with a lid
fork

1. Melt the butter in a saucepan over medium heat. Add the onion. Sauté 5 minutes or until golden brown.

2. Add the bay leaf, cumin and cinnamon. Cook for 1 minute.

3. Add the rice. Cook, stirring constantly, until the rice is transparent.

4. Add the frozen vegetables. Stir. Cook for 1 minute.

5. Add the water, salt, pepper and cayenne pepper. Bring the water to a boil.

6. Cover and reduce the heat to the lowest possible setting. Cook for 20 minutes.

7. Remove the lid and fluff the rice with a fork. Remove the bay leaf before serving.

**Level:
Intermediate**

**Makes:
4 main
course or
6 side dish
servings**

**Preparation:
15 minutes**

**Microwave:
20 minutes**

Risotto

Italian risotto (rih-SOTE-oh) is a creamy rice dish. The usual cooking method takes up to an hour and involves a lot of stirring. This microwave method is fast and easy.

You Will Need

25 mL	butter or margarine	2 tbsp.
25 mL	vegetable oil	2 tbsp.
1	onion, finely chopped	1
500 mL	thinly sliced mushrooms	2 cups
300 mL	arborio rice	1 1/4 cups
625 mL	vegetable stock	2 1/2 cups
125 mL	grated Parmesan cheese	1/2 cup
125 mL	table (18%) cream	1/2 cup
	or	
25 mL	lemon juice	2 tbsp.
25 mL	chopped fresh parsley	2 tbsp.
	salt and pepper to taste	

Utensils

large shallow microwavable dish
measuring cup and spoons

chef's knife
wooden spoon

1. Place butter and oil in a microwavable dish and microwave on high for 1 minute. Stir in onion, mushrooms and rice. Microwave uncovered for 2 minutes.

2. Stir in the vegetable stock. Cook uncovered for 15 to 20 minutes. Once or twice during cooking, remove the dish from the microwave while wearing oven mitts and stir the rice.

3. When the liquid is absorbed and the rice is tender, remove from the microwave. Add Parmesan, cream or lemon juice, parsley, salt and pepper. Stir well. Cover with waxed paper or a paper towel. Let stand 10 minutes. Serve with a sprinkle of Parmesan cheese.

Serving suggestions

Risotto is great on its own with a salad, or as a side dish for Lentil Loaf (page 140) or Baked Tofu (page 136).

Try this!

Instead of mushrooms, try sliced canned artichoke hearts and green olives.

rih SOTE oh oh oh

Basic Pasta and Noodles

Pasta and noodles come in all shapes and sizes. Most are made from semolina, a kind of wheat flour, and some contain other ingredients like herbs or vegetables such as spinach. Pasta made from other grains — spelt, rice, quinoa — is available at specialty bakeries and health food stores.

Long Pasta

▷ spaghetti
▷ spaghettini
▷ vermicelli
▷ fettuccine
▷ lasagna

Short Pasta Shapes

▷ farfalle: bows
▷ conchiglie: shells
▷ rigatoni: tubes
▷ macaroni: small curved tubes
▷ penne: medium straight tubes
▷ cannelloni: big tubes
▷ rotini: spirals

Small Pasta

▷ soup pasta or pastini
▷ couscous

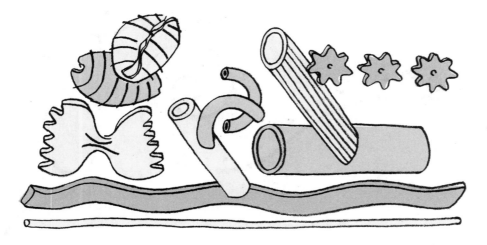

Cooked Pasta

Pasta goes with almost anything, except maybe chocolate sauce. We eat it for lunch and dinner and add it to salads. Follow the instructions on the box or package or use this basic method.

Level:
Beginner
(with help
draining)

Makes:
4 to 6
servings

Preparation:
5 minutes

Cooking:
10 minutes

You Will Need

10 mL	salt	2 tsp.
1 package	pasta	1 package

Utensils

measuring spoons   wooden spoon
bowl   large pot and colander (or pasta pot)

1. Fill a large pot or pasta pot with water. Add the salt. Bring to a boil. Carefully lower the pasta into the water. Stir. When the water boils again, lower the heat to medium and let the pasta cook for 8 to 10 minutes.

2. To test the pasta, carefully remove one piece or strand from the cooking water using a wooden spoon. Let cool slightly. Bite or cut with a fork. It should be soft but not mushy. The Italian term for perfectly cooked pasta is *al dente*, which means "to the tooth."

3. With adult help, drain the pasta in a colander. If you have a pasta pot, lift the strainer out of the pot and let the water drain.

4. Transfer the pasta to a bowl and serve immediately topped with your favorite sauce.

Serving suggestions

Top cooked pasta with Tomato Sauce (page 216) or Pesto (page 218).

Level:
Beginner

Makes:
1 serving

Preparation
and cooking:
15 minutes

Simple Pasta for One

Here's a quick dish that you can make for yourself in no time for lunch or dinner.

You Will Need

4	mushrooms	4
2	green onions	2
1/2	zucchini	1/2
1	clove garlic	1
250 mL	rotini or other small pasta	1 cup
15 mL	olive oil	1 tbsp.
	salt and pepper to taste	
15 mL	grated Parmesan cheese	1 tbsp.

Utensils

measuring cup and spoons
chef's knife
large saucepan

small frying pan
wooden spoon
colander

1. Fill a large saucepan with water. Add a pinch of salt and place over high heat.

2. While the water is coming to a boil, slice the mushrooms, green onions (white and pale green part only) and zucchini. Mince the garlic.

3. When the water boils, add the rotini. Stir. When the water returns to a boil, lower the heat to a simmer and set the timer for 10 minutes.

4. When the timer reaches 5 minutes, heat the oil in a frying pan over medium heat. Add the mushrooms and zucchini. Sauté for 2 minutes. Add the green onions and garlic. Sauté for 3 minutes. Turn off the heat.

5. Drain the rotini in a colander. Pour the cooked rotini into the frying pan with the vegetables. Season with salt and pepper. Toss. Sprinkle with Parmesan cheese and serve.

 Try this!

Substitute any vegetable for those in the recipe. If a vegetable needs more cooking, or is frozen, add it to the pasta as it is cooking. Try broccoli, peas, beans or carrots.

Level:
Beginner

Makes:
500 mL
(2 cups)

Preparation:
2 minutes

Cooking:
2 minutes

Basic Couscous

Couscous is not a grain, as some people imagine, although it does look a bit like cracked wheat. It's a kind of pasta and is common in dishes from North Africa. You can follow the package directions, or use this simple cooking method.

You Will Need

425 mL	vegetable stock or water	1 3/4 cups
2 mL	salt	1/2 tsp.
250 mL	couscous	1 cup

Utensils

saucepan	wooden spoon
measuring cup and spoons	fork

1. In a saucepan, bring vegetable stock and salt to a boil over medium-high heat. Add couscous. Stir. Reduce heat and simmer for 2 minutes or until liquid is absorbed.

2. Remove from heat and fluff with a fork. Let stand for 3 minutes.

Serving suggestions

Top couscous with Curried Vegetables (page 134) or Roasted Root Vegetables (page 210). Or serve as a side dish for Quesadillas (page 62), Tempeh Kabobs (page 138) or Stuffed Pepper Boats (page 148).

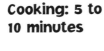

**Level:
Beginner**

**Makes:
4 to 6
servings**

**Preparation:
5 minutes if
using frozen
vegetables**

**Cooking: 5 to
10 minutes**

Mediterranean Couscous

Turn plain couscous into a quick, healthy meal just by adding a few vegetables and some chickpeas.

You Will Need

250 mL	water	1 cup
250 mL	chopped fresh or frozen mixed vegetables	1 cup
250 mL	couscous	1 cup
250 mL	canned chickpeas, rinsed and drained	1 cup

Dressing

25 mL	olive oil	2 tbsp.
15 mL	balsamic vinegar	1 tbsp.
1	clove garlic, minced	1
pinch	dry mustard	pinch

Utensils

measuring cup and spoons
saucepan with a lid
chef's knife

wooden spoon
small jar

1. Place the water and vegetables in a saucepan over high heat. When the water boils, lower the heat and simmer until the vegetables are tender.

2. Add the couscous. Stir. Remove the saucepan from the heat and cover. Let the couscous absorb the water for 5 minutes.

3. Meanwhile, make the dressing. Place all the dressing ingredients in a small jar. Shake well to mix.

4. Stir the couscous to make it fluffy. Add the chickpeas and the dressing. Mix well.

Helpful Hint

This recipe is especially speedy if you use frozen mixed vegetables. Try one of the more unusual mixtures for a change.

Serving suggestions

Serve Mediterranean Couscous as a meal in itself or as a side dish with Vegetarian Burgers (page 126) or Lentil Loaf (page 140).

Breads

Southern Meal

▷ Chili con Elote (page 150)
▷ Cornmeal Bread (page 186)
▷ Twice-Baked Potatoes (page 200)

Movie Night at Home

▷ Spring Rolls (page 66) with dip
▷ Sour Cream and Onion Dip (page 70) with veggies or nachos
▷ Pizza (page 183)
▷ Chocolate Mayonnaise Cupcakes (page 240)

Winter Lunch

▷ Grilled Vegetable Sandwiches (page 54)
on Oatmeal Bread (page 192)
▷ Potato and Cheese Soup (page 88)
▷ Sugar Cookies (page 236)

Pizza or Focaccia Dough

Level:
Intermediate

Makes:
1 focaccia or
1 large pizza

Preparation:
15 minutes

Rising: 1 hour
for pizza,
2 hours for
focaccia

Baking:
20 minutes

dough only

This simple yeast dough can be made into two of our favorite Italian breads: pizza and focaccia (pronounced foe-COTCH-a). After the first rising, you can add toppings — tomato sauce, cheese and other goodies — and bake as a pizza. Or you can sprinkle with salt and toppings, let the dough rise again, and make focaccia. Focaccia can be served as bread to go with a meal, or carefully cut it in half to make a sandwich.

You Will Need

250 mL	warm water	1 cup
1 envelope	yeast	1 envelope
5 mL	sugar	1 tsp.
50 mL	olive oil	3 tbsp.
5 mL	salt	1 tsp.
500 mL	all-purpose flour	2 cups

Utensils

measuring cup and spoons
large mixing bowl
wooden spoon
tea towel

rolling pin
cookie sheet
wire rack

continued

1. In a large mixing bowl, combine the water, yeast and sugar. Stir. Let stand for 5 minutes or until yeast is dissolved.

2. Add the oil, salt and 250 mL (1 cup) of the flour. Stir until well mixed. Add the remaining 250 mL (1 cup) flour, a bit at a time, until the dough begins to break into smaller pieces.

3. Turn the dough out onto a lightly floured surface. Knead (see page 19 for instructions), adding more flour as necessary, for about 5 minutes or until the dough is smooth and it bounces back when gently poked with your fingers.

4. Clean the bowl. Add a few drops of oil. Place the dough in the bowl. Turn it to coat with oil. Cover the bowl with plastic wrap or a damp tea towel. Place in a warm spot to rise until twice the size, about 1 hour.

5. Punch the dough with your fist to push out the air. Turn the dough out onto a lightly floured surface. Knead briefly.

To make focaccia

Pull and stretch the dough with your hands or roll it with a rolling pin until it is about 25 x 45 cm (10 x 18 in.). Grease a cookie sheet. Lift the dough carefully onto the sheet. Brush with 15 mL (1 tbsp.) olive oil. Sprinkle with about 15 mL (1 tbsp.) coarse salt and dried herbs (basil or oregano) or with chopped nuts, grated cheese, sliced olives — almost anything you like. Cover and let rise for another hour or until slightly puffy all over. During the last 15 minutes of the rising time, heat the oven to 180°C (350°F). Poke the dough all over with your fingertips to make small dents. Bake for 20 minutes or until golden brown. Transfer to a wire rack to cool.

To make a pizza

Heat the oven to 220°C (425°F). Sprinkle a little cornmeal on a pizza pan or cookie sheet. Roll the dough flat with a rolling pin. Then stretch and pull it into the shape you want. (You can make one big pizza or several small ones.) Place the dough on the pan. Turn up the edges a bit. Brush the surface with about 15 mL (1 tbsp.) olive oil. (Add a minced clove of garlic to the oil if you like.) Spread a thin layer of tomato sauce and about 250 mL (1 cup) grated mozzarella cheese on top. Add any toppings you like — sun-dried tomatoes, sliced zucchini, tomatoes, onion, olives, mushrooms, capers, broccoli, artichoke hearts, whatever. Sprinkle with Parmesan cheese. Bake for 20 minutes or until dough is browned and cheese is melted.

 Try this!

Instead of tomato sauce, try Pesto (page 218). Instead of or as well as mozzarella, try cheddar or feta cheese.

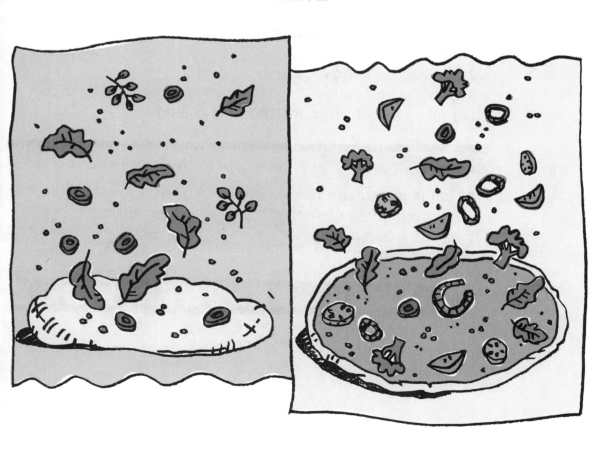

**Level:
Intermediate**

**Makes:
1 pan
(16 pieces)**

**Preparation:
15 minutes**

**Baking:
25 minutes**

Cornmeal Bread

This old-fashioned bread is best served warm, so make it just before you eat it.

You Will Need

125 mL	yellow cornmeal	1/2 cup
250 mL	all-purpose flour	1 cup
50 mL	sugar	1/4 cup
15 mL	baking powder	1 tbsp.
5 mL	salt	1 tsp.
2	eggs	2
375 mL	milk	1 1/2 cups
175 mL	butter, melted and cooled	3/4 cup

Utensils

20 cm (8 in.) square baking pan
measuring cup and spoons
2 mixing bowls

spoon
fork or whisk
wire rack

1. Heat the oven to 200°C (400°F). Grease the baking pan.

2. In a large mixing bowl, combine the cornmeal, flour, sugar, baking powder and salt. Stir.

3. In another mixing bowl, beat the eggs lightly. Add the milk and butter. Mix well.

4. Pour the egg mixture into the cornmeal mixture. Stir until moist. Do not overmix. (Lumps are fine.)

5. Pour the batter into the pan. Bake for 25 minutes or until golden. Let the bread cool slightly.

6. Run a knife around the edge of the pan. Turn the pan upside down over a wire rack and let bread drop onto the rack.

 **Try this!**

Cornmeal Muffins
To make muffins, pour the batter into 12 greased muffin cups. Bake at 200°C (400°F) for 18 to 20 minutes.

Serving suggestions

To serve, cut into squares and put alongside chowder (page 92), stews or Chili con Elote (page 150).

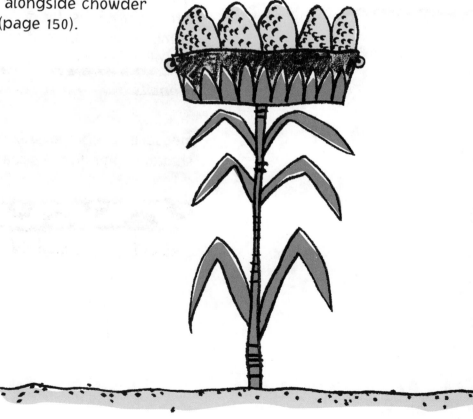

**Level:
Intermediate**

**Makes:
4 servings**

Polenta

**Preparation:
5 minutes**

**Cooking:
15 to 20
minutes**

**with
margarine**

What North Americans call grits or cornmeal mush, Italians call polenta (pronounced POH-len-ta). Whatever you call it, it makes a good side dish or base for sauces and gravies. Serve it as a hot thick mush, or let it set and serve it as a firmer foundation for other foods.

You Will Need

625 mL	cold water	2 1/2 cups
175 mL	yellow cornmeal	3/4 cup
2 mL	salt	1/2 tsp.
15 mL	butter or margarine (optional)	1 tbsp.

Utensils

large saucepan
measuring cup and spoons
shallow 15 cm (6 in.) square pan (if chilling)

whisk
wooden spoon

1. In a large saucepan, combine the water, cornmeal and salt. Whisk until there are no lumps.

2. Bring to a boil over medium heat, stirring frequently. Reduce heat to low. Simmer, stirring constantly, for 10 to 15 minutes or until the polenta leaves a clean path when you scrape the bottom of the pan.

3. Stir in the butter. Cook until melted.

4. Serve immediately or spread in a greased shallow pan to cool for slicing.

 **Try this!**

Add 50 mL (¹⁄₄ cup) Parmesan cheese with the butter in step 3.

Serving suggestions

Serve with Mushroom Gravy (page 220) or Tomato Sauce (page 216).

Fried Polenta

1. Let the polenta cool or chill in a shallow pan. Cut into squares, narrow strips or triangles.

2. To a nonstick frying pan, add 5 mm (¹⁄₄ in.) of vegetable oil. Heat over medium-high heat until oil bubbles when a small piece of polenta is dropped in. Place a few slices of polenta in the pan. Cook 1 to 2 minutes or until the polenta is golden on the bottom. Turn and cook until golden on the other side. Drain on paper towels.

3. Repeat with the remaining slices.

Level:
Intermediate

Makes:
4 servings
or 8 chapatis

Preparation:
15 minutes

Cooking:
15 minutes

Chapatis (or Rotis)

Chapatis are Indian flat breads. They are best served hot, so cook them just before you eat them. You can make the dough earlier, however, and let it rest while you do other things.

You Will Need

250 mL	all-purpose flour	1 cup
250 mL	whole wheat flour	1 cup
5 mL	salt	1 tsp.
10 mL	vegetable oil	2 tsp.
250 mL	hot water	1 cup
	additional oil for cooking	

Utensils

measuring cup and spoons	rolling pin
mixing bowl	heavy frying pan
wooden spoon	spatula
tea towel	knife

1. Place the flours and salt in a mixing bowl. Stir. Drizzle with the oil and mix well. (You can use your fingers for this.)

2. Add about half the hot water. Stir. Drizzle in more water, a bit at a time, stirring well until the flour is moistened. (You may not need all the water.)

3. Form the moistened flour into a ball with your hands. Place on a lightly floured surface. Knead for 10 minutes or until the dough bounces back when you poke it with your fingers. (If you don't want to use the dough right away, wrap it in plastic wrap and put it in the refrigerator.)

4. Cut the dough in half, then cut each half into 4 pieces to make 8 equal pieces. Roll each piece into a ball. Cover with a damp tea towel.

5. Place one ball of dough on a lightly floured surface. Flatten with your hand, then roll with a rolling pin in all directions. Turn the dough over and roll some more, until you have a circle about 15 cm (6 in.) in diameter. Repeat with remaining balls.

6. Heat a frying pan over medium-high heat until a drop of water bounces when dropped on the surface. Add just enough vegetable oil to the pan to make it shine. Place one chapati in the pan. After about 30 seconds, turn it. Press down on the chapati with the spatula. The chapati should begin to puff up slightly. Continue turning and pressing until brown spots appear and the chapati is puffy and cooked, about 2 minutes.

7. Transfer the chapati to paper towels.

8. Repeat with remaining chapatis. You may need to add a bit more oil to the pan. Keep it hot but not smoking.

9. Serve immediately.

Serving suggestions

If you serve chapatis with curry (pages 134 and 157) or Dal (page 222), eat them by tearing off a piece and using it to pick up a bit of food.

If you serve these breads as rotis, place them flat and fill them with mixtures of cooked vegetables and hot sauce. Fold the end up and then the sides over.

**Level:
Advanced**

**Makes:
2 loaves**

**Preparation:
30 minutes**

**Rising: 2 to
2 ½ hours**

**Baking:
45 minutes**

Oatmeal Bread

This bread makes great sandwiches and toast. If you make it with molasses, it will be light brown; with honey it will be whiter. Yeast bread takes a long time to make because of all the time the dough spends rising — you can just leave it alone and do other things.

You Will Need

2 envelopes	yeast	2 envelopes
125 mL	warm water	½ cup
5 mL	sugar	1 tsp.
250 mL	rolled oats	1 cup
125 mL	molasses or honey	½ cup
75 mL	shortening	⅓ cup
15 mL	salt	1 tbsp.
375 mL	boiling water	1 ½ cups
1.5 L	all-purpose flour	6 cups
2	eggs	2

Glaze

1	egg white	1
15 mL	water	1 tbsp.

Utensils

measuring cup and spoons	tea towel
2 small bowls	2 loaf pans
mixing bowl	pastry brush
wooden spoon	wire rack
fork or whisk	knife

1. Place the yeast in a small bowl. Add the warm water and sugar. Stir. Let stand for 10 minutes or until it is foamy.

2. Meanwhile, in a mixing bowl, combine the oats, molasses, shortening and salt. Pour the boiling water on top and stir. Let cool.

3. When the oat mixture is lukewarm, add 1 L (4 cups) of the flour, 500 mL (2 cups) at a time. Beat well after each addition.

4. Beat the eggs in a small bowl. Add the eggs and yeast to the flour mixture. Beat well.

5. Beat in the remaining 500 mL (2 cups) of flour, a little at a time, until the dough comes away from the sides of the bowl. You may not need all the flour.

6. Turn the dough out onto a floured surface. Cover with a damp tea towel and let it rest for 10 minutes.

7. Knead the dough for 5 to 8 minutes or until it is smooth.

8. Clean the mixing bowl and wipe the inside with vegetable oil. Place the dough in the bowl and turn it to coat it with the oil. Cover the bowl with a damp tea towel.

continued

9. Put the bowl in a warm place (on a radiator or in a sunny spot) until the dough is twice the size it was, about 1 ½ hours.

10. With your fist, punch the dough to push out the air.

11. Grease 2 loaf pans thickly with margarine. Sprinkle the insides with about 15 mL (1 tbsp.) of oats.

12. Cut the dough in half. Shape it into 2 loaves. Place the loaves in the pans. Cover with a damp tea towel.

13. Return loaves to a warm spot and let rise until twice the size, 45 to 60 minutes.

14. Heat the oven to 190°C (375°F).

15. To make the glaze, beat the egg white with the water. Brush the tops of the loaves gently with the glaze. Sprinkle lightly with oats.

16. Bake for 45 minutes. If the bread is done it will be golden brown on top and will sound hollow if tapped on the bottom. To do this, wear oven mitts and hold the pan in one hand. Tip the loaf into your other hand. Quickly remove the mitt and tap the bottom of the loaf. If the loaves are done, set them on a rack to cool.

Garlic Bread

Garlic bread is tasty on its own but best of all with spaghetti.

Level:
Beginner

Makes:
4 to 6
servings

Preparation:
10 minutes

Baking: 10 to
15 minutes

You Will Need

50 mL	soft butter	3–4 tbsp.
3	cloves garlic, minced	3
	or	
10 mL	garlic powder	2 tsp.
1 loaf	French or Italian bread	1 loaf
	grated Parmesan cheese	

Utensils

bread knife	small bowl
measuring spoons	cookie sheet
garlic press or chef's knife	spoon

1. Heat the oven to 180°C (350°F).

2. In a small bowl, mix the butter and garlic together.

3. Cut the bread in half lengthwise.

4. Spread the butter and garlic mixture on both halves of the bread. Sprinkle with Parmesan cheese.

5. Close the two halves of the bread. Place on a long sheet of foil. Wrap bread and seal the foil. Place on a cookie sheet.

6. Bake for 10 to 15 minutes. Wearing oven mitts, remove from the oven. Remove foil, watching out for escaping steam.

7. When the bread is cool enough to handle, slice it into 5-cm (2-in.) pieces.

Try this!

▷ **Another way to cut**
You can also slice the bread diagonally to start. Make your cuts down to, but not through, the bottom crust. Open each cut and spread a little garlic butter between the slices. Wrap in foil and heat in the oven as above.

▷ **Herb Garlic Bread**
Add some oregano or basil or both to the garlic butter.

Vegetables

Light Lunch or Quick Dinner

▷ Potato Pancakes (page 206) with applesauce or sour cream
▷ Green Salad (page 101) with Vinaigrette Dressing (page 103)
▷ More Than Peanut Butter Cookies (page 230)

Caribbean Dinner

▷ Cuban Black Bean Soup (page 96)
▷ Chickpea Curry (page 157) with Rotis (page 190)
▷ Fried Plantains (page 209)
▷ Fresh Fruit Salad (page 227)

Barbecue for a Crowd

▷ Creamy Tomato Soup (page 98)
▷ Tempeh Kabobs (page 138) with Yogurt Sauce (page 125)
▷ Vegetarian Burgers (page 126)
▷ Corn on the cob (page 198)
▷ Pasta Salad with Mixed Vegetables (page 110)
▷ Apple Upside-Down Cake (page 244)
▷ Brownies (page 238)

Basic Vegetables

You can do almost anything with vegetables. You can steam, microwave, roast, sauté or boil them. And you can even eat most of them raw. However you eat them, first wash or peel them and cut them into equal-sized pieces.

Steaming

It is much better to steam most vegetables than to boil them. Boiled vegetables don't taste as fresh and aren't as good for you since lots of the vitamins end up in the water. Put about 5 cm (2 in.) of water in a saucepan. Place the steamer in the saucepan. Place the vegetables in the steamer. Bring the water to a boil. Reduce heat to a simmer. Cover the saucepan. Cook until tender.

Microwaving

Put vegetables in a microwavable dish with about 50 mL (¼ cup) water. Cover and microwave on high until tender.

Boiling

Place vegetables in just enough water to cover them. Bring the water to a boil. Simmer until tender. Drain well.

Sautéing and stir-frying

Many vegetables are best sautéed or stir-fried. Cooking without water keeps the flavor and goodness in the food and gives it a nice crispness. Mushrooms and zucchini are wonderful sliced and sautéed in a little oil or butter. Some vegetables can be boiled or steamed briefly first and then sautéed or added to stir-fries.

continued

Vegetable	Steam or boil	Microwave
Artichokes	45 minutes to 1 hour	8 to 10 minutes
Asparagus	5 to 10 minutes	8 minutes for 500 g (1 lb.)
Beans	5 to 10 minutes	4 to 8 minutes
Beets	40 minutes to 1 hour	10 minutes for 500 g (1 lb.)
Broccoli	3 to 12 minutes	5 minutes
Brussels sprouts	8 to 12 minutes	2 to 8 minutes, depending on size
Cabbage	5 to 10 minutes	4 to 7 minutes
Carrots	5 to 10 minutes	4 to 6 minutes
Cauliflower	8 to 15 minutes	6 to 8 minutes
Corn	7 to 10 minutes	see below
Greens	see below	see below
Peas	3 to 5 minutes	5 to 10 minutes
String beans	3 to 5 minutes	4 to 8 minutes

Greens

To cook tender greens like spinach, Swiss chard, and beet greens, wash the leaves well and remove any tough or stringy bits. Do not dry the greens. Place them in a saucepan with the water still on the leaves. Do not add any more water. Cover and heat for 2 to 3 minutes or until the greens are wilted. Drain well and chop.

To cook spinach in the microwave, put the washed leaves in a microwavable container. Sprinkle with just a little water. Cover and microwave for about 3 minutes or until the leaves wilt.

Tougher greens like kale require longer cooking times — 4 to 5 minutes — and can be boiled or steamed.

Corn in the microwave

To cook corn in the microwave, wet the unhusked corn under cold water. Put one ear of corn, husk and all, into the microwave and cook on high for 4 to 5 minutes. Wearing oven mitts, remove corn from the microwave. Carefully remove the husk. The silk will come away with it.

Fancier Vegetables

Glazed Carrots

Put cooked carrots in a saucepan. Add 15 mL (1 tbsp.) brown sugar and 15 mL (1 tbsp.) butter or margarine. Stir until butter is melted and carrots are coated.

Green Beans with Almonds

To cooked beans, add 15 mL (1 tbsp.) butter and 50 mL (¼ cup) slivered almonds. Stir until butter is melted.

Cauliflower with Cheese Sauce

Pour Cheese Sauce (page 213) over cooked cauliflower.

**Level:
Intermediate**

**Makes:
1 serving**

**Preparation
and Cooking:
1 hour and
15 minutes
(in the oven)**

**10 minutes
per potato
(in the
microwave)**

Try this!

In the microwave
Pierce the potato with a fork in a few places. Bake for 3 to 4 minutes per potato in the microwave, then make filling as described above. After step 4, place the potatoes on a plate. Microwave on high for 1 minute per potato.

Twice-Baked Potato

Baked potatoes are a vegetarian's standby. They are delicious with butter or sour cream on top, but here's a way to make them even better and add some extra protein at the same time.

You Will Need

1	potato	1
25 mL	butter or margarine	2 tbsp.
25 mL	sour cream or tofu mayonnaise (page 214)	2 tbsp.
	salt and pepper to taste	
50 mL	grated cheddar cheese	1/4 cup

Utensils

fork
chef's knife
small spoon
mixing bowl

measuring cup and spoons
cookie sheet
electric mixer or potato masher
grater

1. Heat oven to 180°C (350°F). Scrub the potato and pierce the skin a couple times with a fork. Bake for 40 minutes to 1 hour or until soft when squeezed. Remove from the oven and let cool.

2. When the baked potato is cool enough to handle, slice it in half lengthwise. With a small spoon, scoop out the center of the potato and place in a mixing bowl. Leave the potato skin intact.

3. Add the butter, sour cream, salt and pepper. With an electric mixer or potato masher, mix until smooth.

4. Spoon the potato mixture back into the shell. Sprinkle cheese on top.

5. Place the potato on a cookie sheet and bake for 10 minutes or until heated through and the cheese has melted.

 Try this!

Add a little sautéed onion to the mashed potato for more zing.

Twice-Baked Sweet Potatoes

Substitute sweet potatoes for the regular potatoes. Mash them with a pinch of brown sugar instead of sour cream and top with a spoonful of leftover chili.

**Level:
Intermediate**

**Makes:
4 servings**

**Preparation:
15 minutes**

**Cooking:
20 minutes**

**with soy
milk and
margarine
or tofu
mayonnaise**

Mashed Potatoes

Mashed potatoes go with almost anything.

You Will Need

3–4	peeled potatoes, cut in chunks	3–4
125 mL	milk or soy milk	½ cup
50 mL	butter, margarine or tofu mayonnaise (page 214)	3 tbsp.
	salt and pepper to taste	

Utensils

measuring cup and spoons   colander
potato masher or electric mixer   potato peeler
large saucepan   chef's knife

1. Place the potatoes in a large saucepan. Add enough cold water to cover them. Bring water to a boil. Reduce heat and simmer for 15 to 20 minutes or until potatoes are tender when poked with a fork.

2. Drain the potatoes in a colander. Return the potatoes to the saucepan.

3. Mash the potatoes until smooth with a potato masher or electric mixer.

4. Gradually add milk, butter, salt and pepper, mashing potatoes until fluffy.

Helpful Hint

If the potatoes are old, add a pinch or two of sugar with the salt and pepper.

Serving suggestion

Serve mashed potatoes plain with butter, salt and pepper or topped with Mushroom Gravy (page 220).

 **Try this!**

Steam or sauté some chopped greens, such as spinach, cabbage or kale. Drain the greens well and add them to the mashed potatoes for extra flavor and goodness — and a nice green color. Call the dish colcannon, an old Irish name, and impress your family.

Oven-Fried Potatoes

Makes:
4 servings

Preparation:
15 minutes

Here's a great substitute for French fries that you don't have to deep fry.

Cooking:
40 minutes

You Will Need

5	potatoes	5
25 mL	vegetable oil	2 tbsp.
	salt and pepper to taste	

Utensils

measuring spoons	large bowl
chef's knife	cookie sheet
saucepan	spatula
colander	

1. Heat the oven to 200°C (400°F).

2. Scrub the potatoes. (Do not peel them unless they are very old or very dirty.) Cut into 8 wedges.

3. Place the potato wedges in a saucepan. Add enough water to just cover. Bring to a boil. Reduce heat and simmer for 8 minutes. Do not overcook. Drain the potatoes in a colander.

4. Place the potatoes in a large bowl. Sprinkle with oil, salt and pepper. Toss. Place seasoned potatoes on a cookie sheet in a single layer. Bake for 15 minutes. Remove from the oven. Turn the potatoes with a spatula. Bake for another 15 minutes or until crispy.

 **Try this!**

▷ **Chili Fries**

Place the drained potatoes in a bowl. Sprinkle with 25 mL (2 tbsp.) flour and 5 mL (1 tsp.) chili powder. Toss gently with a wooden spoon. Continue with step 4.

▷ **Italian Fries**

Sprinkle with oregano or Italian seasoning in step 4.

Level:
Intermediate

Makes:
4 servings

Preparation:
15 to 20 minutes

Cooking:
20 minutes

Potato Pancakes (Latkes)

Potato pancakes make a quick, light lunch or dinner. Judi's daughter, Emma, makes these when time is short and the cupboard is almost bare.

You Will Need

3–4	potatoes	3–4
1	small onion (optional)	1
1	egg	1
15 mL	all-purpose flour	1 tbsp.
15 mL	milk or cream	1 tbsp.
	salt and pepper to taste	
15 mL	vegetable oil	1 tbsp.

Utensils

measuring spoons
mixing bowl
potato peeler
nonstick frying pan
grater

fork
small bowl
spoon
spatula

1. Peel the potatoes and onion. Place a grater in a mixing bowl and grate the potatoes and onion. Pour off any liquid.

2. Break the egg into a small bowl. Beat it, then add to the potatoes.

3. Add the flour, milk, salt and pepper. Mix well.

4. Heat the oil in a nonstick frying pan over medium heat until it sizzles.

5. Carefully spoon the potato batter into the pan by the spoonfuls. Flatten each pancake with a spatula.

6. When pancakes are golden brown underneath, carefully turn them over using a spatula. Fry on the other side until brown and crisp.

7. Put 3 or 4 paper towels on a plate. When pancakes are done, place them on the plate to remove extra oil. Don't stack them on top of each other or they will get soggy.

Helpful Hint

If making a lot of latkes, keep them warm in the oven at 120°C (250°F), but they are best when eaten right away. Don't stack them; they will get soggy. Instead, put them on a plate in a single layer.

Serving suggestions

Serve with applesauce and sour cream as toppings and a salad on the side.

 **Try this!**

Add 50 mL (¼ cup) grated zucchini.

**Level:
Intermediate
(with help)**

**Makes:
4 servings**

**Preparation:
5 minutes**

**Cooking:
1 hour**

**with
margarine**

Baked Squash

When we have baked squash to go with a meat dish for the rest of the family, the vegetarians enjoy an extra serving of squash.

You Will Need

2	acorn squash	2
50 mL	butter or margarine	4 tbsp.
50 mL	brown sugar	4 tbsp.

Utensils

measuring spoons   spatula
chef's knife   spoon
cookie sheet

1. Heat the oven to 180°C (350°F).

2. Cut the squashes in half from stem end to bottom end. Scoop out the seeds.

3. Place the halves cut side down on a cookie sheet. Bake for 30 minutes.

4. Wearing oven mitts, remove the cookie sheet from the oven. Using a spatula, turn the squash halves over. Spoon the butter and sugar into the hollows of the squash. Bake for another 30 minutes or until the squash is soft. Let stand for 5 minutes before serving.

Helpful Hint

Winter squashes like acorn squash have hard rinds that are tough to cut. Ask an adult to help.

Fried Plantains

These are simple to prepare and are an excellent addition to any meal. Ripe plantains have black spots on the outside.

Level:
Beginner

Makes:
4 servings

Preparation:
5 minutes

Cooking:
10 to 15 minutes

You Will Need

25 mL	vegetable oil	2 tbsp.
2	plantains, peeled and sliced on the diagonal	2
	salt to taste	

Utensils

nonstick frying pan
chef's knife

measuring spoons
spatula

1. In a nonstick frying pan, heat the oil over medium-high heat. Add some of the plantains in a single layer. Cook for about 3 minutes or until golden brown on the bottom. Turn and cook on the other side until golden brown. Drain on paper towels.

2. Repeat with remaining slices.

Serving suggestions

Serve with a curry (pages 134 or 157) or Veggie Stir-Fry (page 130).

Level:
Intermediate

Makes:
4 to 6
servings

Preparation:
20 minutes

Cooking:
1 hour to
1 hour and
10 minutes

Roasted Root Vegetables

Here's a great winter dish that can be made with all or some of the vegetables listed — or add your favorites.

You Will Need

1	onion	1
2	parsnips, peeled	2
2	carrots	2
1	Yukon Gold potato, scrubbed	1
1	sweet potato, peeled	1
1	butternut squash, peeled	1
5	cloves garlic	5
75 mL	olive oil	1/3 cup
	salt and freshly ground pepper to taste	

Utensils

measuring cup
chef's knife
large roasting pan

wooden spoon
potato peeler

1. Heat oven to 180°C (350°F).

2. Cut the onion into 8 wedges. Cut the parsnips and carrots on the diagonal into 5-mm (1/4-in.) slices. Cut the potato and sweet potato into 5-cm (1/4-in.) slices. Cut the squash into 1-cm (1/2-in.) slices.

3. Put all the vegetables and the garlic in a large roasting pan. Add the olive oil. Season with salt and pepper. Toss well. Cover with a lid or foil. Bake for 30 minutes.

4. Uncover and bake, stirring occasionally, for 30 to 40 minutes or until vegetables are tender, golden brown and still slightly crisp.

Sauces and Fillings

Family Dinner

▷Lentil Loaf (page 140) with Mushroom Gravy (page 220)
▷Baked Squash (page 208)
▷Green Salad (page 101) with Blue Cheese Dressing (page 103)
▷Rice Pudding (page 246)

Brunch

▷Fresh fruit
▷Breakfast Burrito (page 38)
▷Refried Beans (page 224)
▷Tropical Tofu Frostie (page 252)

Light Dinner

▷Red Lentil Soup (page 87)
▷Stuffed Portobello Mushrooms (page 128) on a bun
▷Fresh fruit

White Sauce

Sauces make an ordinary cooked vegetable special.

Level:
Intermediate

Makes:
250 mL
(1 cup)

Preparation:
5 minutes

Cooking:
5 minutes

You Will Need

25 mL	butter or margarine	2 tbsp.
25 mL	all-purpose flour	2 tbsp.
250 mL	milk	1 cup
	salt and pepper to taste	

Utensils

measuring cup and spoons   wooden spoon or whisk
small saucepan

1. Heat the butter in a small saucepan over medium-high heat until it foams.

2. Add the flour slowly, while stirring, until thoroughly mixed. Remove the pan from the heat.

3. Add the milk slowly, while stirring. Stir until there are no lumps.

4. Cook over medium-high heat, stirring constantly, until the sauce has thickened. Add salt and pepper. Reduce heat and simmer for 3 minutes.

✿ Try this!

▷ **Cheese Sauce**
With the salt and pepper, add 50 mL (¹/₄ cup) grated cheese.

▷ **Parsley Sauce**
Before serving, add 25 mL (2 tbsp.) chopped fresh parsley and 25 mL (2 tbsp.) lemon juice.

Serving suggestions

White sauce makes any vegetable creamy. Stir in cooked peas, green beans, boiled onions, corn or chopped spinach. Or use it as the base for other sauces.

**Level:
Beginner**

**Makes:
250 mL
(1 cup)**

**Preparation:
5 minutes**

Tofu Mayonnaise

Here's a vegan mayonnaise that tops the original version.

You Will Need

175 g (1/2 box)	silken tofu	6 oz. (1/2 box)
75 mL	olive oil	1/3 cup
1	clove garlic, chopped	1
25 mL	lemon juice	2 tbsp.
10 mL	Dijon mustard	2 tsp.
1 mL	salt	1/4 tsp.
	white pepper to taste	

Utensils

measuring cup and spoons
chef's knife
juicer

food processor or blender
rubber scraper
bowl

1. Place the tofu and oil in a food processor or blender. Blend for 30 seconds or until smooth.

2. Add the garlic, lemon juice, mustard, salt and pepper. Blend for 15 seconds. Scrape into a bowl and refrigerate until ready to use.

Serving suggestions

Keep a jar of this mayonnaise in the fridge and add some to Potato Salad (page 112), spread it on bread for sandwiches, or mix a little in with your vegetables.

Peanut Sauce

This thick sauce has lots of uses — as a dipping sauce, as a topping for noodles or as a spread in wraps.

You Will Need

250 mL	unsalted roasted peanuts	1 cup
175 mL	coconut milk	3/4 cup
25 mL	soy sauce	2 tbsp.
15 mL	ground coriander	1 tbsp.
15 mL	dark brown sugar	1 tbsp.

Utensils

measuring cup and spoons   small frying pan
blender or food processor   wooden spoon

1. In a blender or food processor, grind the peanuts just until they are in small pieces.

2. Place the peanuts, coconut milk, soy sauce, coriander and sugar in a small frying pan. Cook over low heat, stirring, for 4 minutes.

Level:
Beginner

Makes:
1.2 to 1.5 L
(5 to 6 cups)

Preparation:
15 to 20
minutes

Cooking:
1 ½ hours

Try this!

▷ **Tomato and Mushroom Sauce**

After the onions and garlic have cooked, add 10 to 12 sliced mushrooms. Sauté for 3 minutes. Continue with step 2.

Tomato Sauce

Tomato sauce makes a simple topping for pasta. You can also add other ingredients to suit your taste.

You Will Need

15 mL	olive oil	1 tbsp.
1	onion, chopped	1
2	cloves garlic, minced	2
2 796-mL cans	crushed tomatoes	2 28-oz. cans
1 156-mL can	tomato paste	1 5.5-oz. can
10 mL	dried basil	2 tsp.
	salt and pepper to taste	

Utensils

chef's knife
measuring cup and spoons

large pot
wooden spoon

1. In a large pot, heat the oil over medium heat. Add the onion. Sauté for 3 to 5 minutes or until the onion is tender. Add the garlic. Sauté for 1 minute.

2. Add the tomatoes, tomato paste, basil, salt and pepper. Bring to a boil. Reduce heat to a simmer and cook for 1 ½ hours. Stir occasionally.

3. Pour the sauce over cooked pasta and top with Parmesan cheese.

Hollandaise Sauce

Level:
Advanced

Makes:
250 mL
(1 cup)

Preparation:
5 minutes

This wonderful rich sauce brings a touch of class to any vegetable. Pour it over a poached egg on an English muffin.

You Will Need

3	egg yolks	3
15 mL	lemon juice	1 tbsp.
1 mL	salt	¼ tsp.
dash	cayenne pepper (optional)	dash
125 mL	butter	½ cup

Utensils

measuring spoons	knife
juicer	blender
small saucepan or glass measuring cup	

1. Place the egg yolks, lemon juice, salt and cayenne in a blender. Process for 5 seconds or until smooth. Open the hole in the blender lid.

2. Heat the butter to boiling in a small saucepan or in a glass measuring cup in the microwave. (Microwave for 1 minute and 30 seconds or until it is bubbling.)

3. Immediately turn the blender on. Slowly pour in the boiling butter. The hot butter will cook the eggs and thicken the sauce. Let the blender run for about 1 minute or until the sauce is creamy.

Serving suggestions

Pour over any cooked vegetable, or dip artichoke leaves in one at a time and strip the soft part off with your teeth.

Helpful Hint

To separate an egg, carefully crack it open. Hold one half of the shell in each hand, facing up. The yolk will be in one half. Pour the white of the egg from the other half into a bowl. Now slide the yolk into the empty shell, and pour the white from the other half. Be careful not to break the yolk.

Level:
Intermediate

Makes:
250 mL
(1 cup)

Preparation:
10 minutes

Pesto

This Italian sauce is usually spooned over pasta and tossed to coat. It can also be added to soups or even just spread on crackers. Pesto is easy to make in a blender or food processor.

You Will Need

750 mL	packed basil leaves	3 cups
125 mL	olive oil	1/2 cup
50 mL	pine nuts	3 tbsp.
5 mL	salt	1 tsp.
2	cloves garlic, chopped	2
125 mL	grated Parmesan cheese	1/2 cup

Utensils

food processor or blender
rubber scraper

mixing bowl
chef's knife

1. Wash the basil leaves. Dry them on a tea towel or in a salad spinner. They must be completely dry.

2. Place the basil, oil, pine nuts, salt and garlic in a food processor or blender. Process for 1 minute or until smooth. You may need to stop and push the ingredients down once or twice during processing.

3. Scrape the mixture into a mixing bowl. Stir in the cheese.

4. To serve, place 15 to 25 mL (1 to 2 tbsp.) pesto on each serving of pasta. Toss well to mix. Sprinkle with more Parmesan if you like.

Helpful Hint

Pesto can be frozen before the cheese is added. Whip up lots in the summer when fresh basil is plentiful. Spoon it into small containers or ice cube trays. Thaw, then add fresh cheese.

 **Try this!**

▷ Substitute walnuts or almonds for the pine nuts.
▷ Substitute parsley for some of the basil.
▷ Substitute fresh spinach for the basil.

Level:
Intermediate

Makes:
about
625 mL
(2 ½ cups)

Preparation:
10 minutes

Cooking:
20 minutes

Mushroom Gravy

This is so-so-so good!

You Will Need

14	mushrooms, halved	14
50 mL	olive oil	4 tbsp.
1	onion, finely chopped	1
25 mL	whole wheat flour	2 tbsp.
500 mL	vegetable stock or water	2 cups
5 mL	soy sauce	1 tsp.
5 mL	vegetarian Worcestershire sauce	1 tsp.
1 mL	dried thyme, sage or Italian seasoning	¼ tsp.
2 mL	salt	½ tsp.
	freshly ground pepper to taste	

Utensils

food processor
chef's knife
measuring cup and spoons

large frying pan
spatula
wooden spoon

1. Put the mushrooms in a food processor. Process until mushrooms are very finely chopped, scraping down the sides if necessary. Set aside.

2. In a large frying pan, heat 25 mL (2 tbsp.) of the oil over medium-high heat. Add the onion. Sauté for 5 to 7 minutes or until very tender.

3. Add the mushrooms. Sauté for 5 minutes or until most of the liquid has evaporated.

4. Push the mushrooms to the edge of pan. Add 25 mL (2 tbsp.) of the oil and the flour to the center of pan. Cook the flour mixture for 1 minute, stirring constantly.

5. Add the stock, stirring constantly until the flour mixture is dissolved. Add the soy sauce, Worcestershire sauce, thyme, salt and pepper. Stir. Bring the gravy to a boil. Stir everything together. Reduce heat and simmer gently for 5 minutes. Taste and correct seasoning before serving.

Serving suggestions

Serve with Mashed (page 202) or Oven-Fried Potatoes (page 204) or over Lentil Loaf (page 140) or Polenta (page 188).

Level:
Intermediate

Makes:
6 servings

Preparation:
20 minutes

Cooking:
30 minutes

Dal

Dal is an Indian specialty that can be served as a topping or a soup. Make a lot and keep it in the fridge for quick lunches or dinners.

You Will Need

25 mL	olive oil	2 tbsp.
1/2	onion, chopped	1/2
1	clove garlic, minced	1
5 mL	grated gingerroot	1 tsp.
125 mL	tomato paste	1/2 cup
5 mL	curry paste	1 tsp.
5 mL	ground coriander	1 tsp.
5 mL	ground cumin	1 tsp.
250 mL	dried red lentils	1 cup
1 398-mL can	coconut milk	1 14-oz. can
500 mL	water	2 cups
	salt to taste	

Utensils

measuring cup and spoons
chef's knife
wooden spoon

grater
large saucepan with a lid

1. Heat the oil in a large saucepan over medium heat. Add the onion, garlic and ginger. Sauté for 5 minutes or until the onion is soft.

2. Add the tomato paste, curry paste, coriander and cumin. Cook for 3 minutes, stirring constantly.

3. Add the lentils, coconut milk and water. Stir to mix well. Increase heat and continue to cook until the mixture boils. Reduce heat to low. Partially cover the saucepan and cook for 20 minutes stirring occasionally, until the dal thickens. Stir in salt.

Serving suggestions

Serve with rice or in sandwich wraps.

 **Try this!**

▷ Add 250 to 500 mL (1 to 2 cups) vegetables — corn or chopped carrots or celery — to the dal for the last 10 minutes of cooking time.

▷ **Dal Soup**
Add 250 mL (1 cup) or more unsweetened coconut milk.

Level:
Intermediate

Makes:
500 mL
(2 cups)

Preparation:
10 minutes

Cooking:
35 minutes

Refried Beans

These beans are only fried once, so they should probably be called just fried beans. Maybe someone thought that sounded boring. Whether the name makes sense or not, these beans are good for you and extremely versatile.

You Will Need

15 mL	vegetable oil	1 tbsp.
1	onion, finely chopped	1
1	clove garlic, finely chopped	1
1 540-mL can	kidney or black beans, rinsed and drained	1 19-oz. can
250 mL	vegetable stock	1 cup
10 mL	ground coriander	2 tsp.
15 mL	seeded and finely chopped jalapeño pepper	1 tbsp.
15 mL	chopped parsley (optional) salt and pepper to taste	1 tbsp.

Utensils

colander
chef's knife
measuring cup and spoons
nonstick frying pan

wooden spoon
bowl
potato masher

1. Heat the oil in a nonstick frying pan over medium heat. Add the onion. Sauté for 2 to 3 minutes or until onion is tender. Add the garlic and sauté for 1 minute more.

2. Add the beans, vegetable stock, coriander, jalapeño pepper, parsley, salt and pepper. Simmer for 20 minutes.

3. Remove 250 mL (1 cup) of the beans from the pan and place them in a bowl. Mash them until they form a paste. Return them to the pan. Stir.

Serving suggestion

Serve these beans in burritos, tacos or rotis, as a dip with nachos or just by themselves.

Helpful Hint

Immediately after cutting the jalapeño pepper, wash your hands really well. The oils from the pepper can be very painful if they get in your eyes.

Cookies and Desserts

Breakfast for Dinner

▷ Cheese Omelet (page 34)
▷ Oven-Fried Potatoes (page 204)
▷ Banana-Chocolate Delight (page 229)
▷ Milk or juice

Sail Away Dinner

▷ Stuffed Pepper Boats (page 148)
▷ Couscous (page 178)
▷ Carrot and Raisin Salad (page 115)
▷ Apple Upside-Down Cake (page 244)

Gifts

▷ Sugar Cookies (page 236)
▷ Curried Nuts (page 73)
▷ Apple Walnut Loaf (page 44)

Fresh Fruit Salad

Level:
Beginner

Makes:
4 to 6
servings

Go to the store and pick out your favorite fruits for this classic dessert. Fresh fruit in season makes the best fruit salad. Don't forget to wash all fruit before cutting it.

Preparation:
15 to 20
minutes

without
marshmallows

You Will Need

250 mL	blueberries	1 cup
250 mL	strawberries, hulls removed	1 cup
500 mL	cubed melon (honeydew, cantaloupe or seedless watermelon)	2 cups
250 mL	cubed pineapple	1 cup
2	kiwi, peeled and sliced	2
125 mL	orange juice	1/2 cup
125 mL	miniature marshmallows	1/2 cup
25 mL	shredded sweetened coconut	2 tbsp.

Utensils

chef's knife
measuring cup and spoons

large bowl
spoons

1. Combine all the fruit in a large bowl. Add the orange juice and toss gently. Refrigerate until ready to serve.

2. Just before serving, add the marshmallows and coconut. Stir gently.

Level:
Beginner

Makes:
4 servings

Preparation:
10 minutes

Freezing:
2 to 3 hours

 Try this!

Try other combinations of fruit: strawberry and banana, or raspberry and banana.

Peach-Banana Sorbet

Enjoy this thick, creamy, all-natural sorbet on a hot summer's day.

You Will Need

1	banana, cut in chunks	1
2	peach, peeled and cut in chunks	2
125 mL	peach nectar	½ cup
25 mL	honey or maple syrup	2 tbsp.
15 mL	lemon juice	1 tbsp.

Utensils

juicer
cookie sheet
chef's knife

blender or food processor
measuring cup and spoons

1. Line a cookie sheet with waxed paper. Place the chunks of banana and peach on the cookie sheet and freeze for 2 to 3 hours.

2. Just before serving, place the fruit in a blender and blend until well mixed. Add the peach nectar, honey and lemon juice. Blend until thick and creamy. Serve immediately.

Banana-Chocolate Delight

Level:
Beginner

Makes:
4 servings

Preparation:
5 minutes

Baking:
10 minutes

This dessert can be made in minutes when you are in a hurry. If you can't finish it all, it tastes even better cold the next day.

You Will Need

4	small bananas, thinly sliced crosswise	4
250 mL	semisweet chocolate chips	1 cup
125 mL	heavy (35%) cream	1/2 cup
2 mL	vanilla	1/2 tsp.

Utensils

4 250-mL (1-cup) ramekins	cookie sheet
small bowl	paring knife
spoon	measuring cup and spoons

Ramekins are small bowls with straight sides that can go in the oven and to the table.

1. Heat the oven to 220°C (425°F).

2. Cover the bottom of each ramekin with the slices from one banana. Sprinkle one-quarter of the chocolate chips over each.

3. In a small bowl, stir together the cream and vanilla. Pour over the bananas and chocolate chips. Put the ramekins on a cookie sheet. Bake for 10 minutes.

**Level:
Intermediate**

**Makes:
24 cookies**

**Preparation:
20 to 25
minutes**

**Baking:
25 minutes
(for 2
batches)**

More Than Peanut Butter Cookies

These cookies are dairy-free and egg-free. If you use honey, or a blend of honey and maple syrup, gently heat the honey in a small saucepan.

You Will need

250 mL	natural chunky or smooth peanut butter	1 cup
250 mL	maple syrup, honey or a blend of both	1 cup
125 mL	applesauce	1/2 cup
	or	
1	banana, mashed	1
50 mL	vegetable oil	3 tbsp.
7 mL	vanilla	1 1/2 tsp.
625 mL	whole wheat pastry flour	2 1/2 cups
5 mL	baking powder	1 tsp.
5 mL	baking soda	1 tsp.
2 mL	salt	1/2 tsp.
250 mL	semisweet chocolate chips	1 cup

Utensils

2 mixing bowls	measuring cup and spoons
whisk	cookie sheet
wooden spoon	fork

1. Heat the oven to 180°C (350°F). Grease a cookie sheet and lightly dust it with flour.

2. In a mixing bowl, whisk the peanut butter, maple syrup, applesauce, vegetable oil and vanilla until smooth.

3. In another mixing bowl, mix the flour, baking powder, baking soda and salt. Make a well in the center of the dry mixture. Pour in the liquid mixture, stirring just until blended. Add chocolate chips. Stir.

4. Using your hands, shape the dough into 4-cm (1 ½-in.) balls. Place on the cookie sheet 6 cm (2 ½ in.) apart. Dip a fork into a little flour and press down on the balls two or three times, flattening them to 1 cm (½ in.) thick.

5. Bake for 10 to 12 minutes or until lightly browned. Remove the cookies from the cookie sheet using oven mitts and a spatula. Carefully place them on a wire rack to cool.

Level:
Intermediate

Makes:
36 cookies

Preparation:
20 minutes

Baking:
15 minutes

Pumpkin Cookies

Pumpkins give us pie for Thanksgiving and jack-o'-lanterns for Halloween. Here's a way to turn them into tasty and nutritious cookies as well. Use canned pure pumpkin purée, not pumpkin pie filling.

You Will Need

500 mL	all-purpose flour	2 cups
250 mL	oats	1 cup
5 mL	baking soda	1 tsp.
5 mL	cinnamon	1 tsp.
2 mL	salt	1/2 tsp.
175 mL	butter or margarine	3/4 cup
250 mL	firmly packed brown sugar	1 cup
125 mL	white sugar	1/2 cup
1	egg	1
2 mL	vanilla	1/2 tsp.
250 mL	canned pumpkin purée	1 cup
250 mL	raisins	1 cup
125 mL	chopped walnuts (optional)	1/2 cup

Utensils

2 mixing bowls
measuring cup and spoons
wooden spoon

cookie sheet
wire rack

1. Heat the oven to 180°C (350°F). Grease a cookie sheet.

2. In a mixing bowl, combine the flour, oats, baking soda, cinnamon and salt. Stir.

3. In another mixing bowl, cream the butter and both sugars with a wooden spoon until smooth.

4. Add the egg and vanilla. Beat until smooth.

5. Add 125 mL (½ cup) of the flour mixture and then 50 mL (¼ cup) of the pumpkin purée. Stir. Repeat until all the flour and purée have been added.

6. Stir in the raisins and nuts until blended.

7. Drop by the tablespoon onto a greased cookie sheet 2.5 cm (1 in.) apart. Bake for 12 to 15 minutes or until golden. Remove the cookies from the cookie sheet using oven mitts and a spatula. Carefully place them on a wire rack to cool.

Level:
Beginner

Makes:
30 cookies

Preparation:
25 minutes

Baking:
40 minutes
(for 2
batches)

Maple Oat Cookies

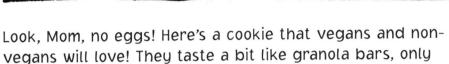

Look, Mom, no eggs! Here's a cookie that vegans and non-vegans will love! They taste a bit like granola bars, only better, and keep well in an airtight container.

You Will Need

250 mL	whole wheat flour	1 cup
250 mL	rolled oats	1 cup
150 mL	brown sugar	$2/3$ cup
5 mL	baking soda	1 tsp.
2 mL	cinnamon	$1/2$ tsp.
2 mL	nutmeg	$1/2$ tsp.
50 mL	maple syrup	$1/4$ cup
50 mL	water	$1/4$ cup
5 mL	vanilla	1 tsp.
125 mL	raisins	$1/2$ cup
75 mL	walnuts (optional)	$1/3$ cup

Utensils

2 mixing bowls
measuring cup and spoons
wooden spoon

cookie sheet
spatula
wire rack

1. Heat the oven to 140°C (275°F). Grease a cookie sheet really well.

2. In a mixing bowl, combine the flour, oats, sugar, baking soda, cinnamon and nutmeg. Stir.

3. In another bowl, combine the maple syrup, water and vanilla. Add to the flour mixture. Mix well. Stir in the raisins and walnuts.

4. With your hands, form the dough into small balls about 2.5 cm (1 in.) across. Place on the cookie sheet 4 cm (1 ½ in.) apart. Flatten slightly with the back of the wooden spoon. Bake 20 minutes or until light brown.

5. Let cool on the cookie sheet for 2 minutes, then transfer to a wire rack to cool completely.

Level:
Intermediate

Makes:
48 cookies

Preparation:
20 minutes

Chilling:
1 hour

Baking:
40 minutes
(for 4
batches)

Sugar Cookies

Leave these cookies plain or decorate them for a special holiday. You can make different shapes by using different cookie cutters.

You Will Need

175 mL	shortening	3/4 cup
250 mL	sugar	1 cup
2	eggs	2
5 mL	vanilla	1 tsp.
	or	
2 mL	lemon extract	1/2 tsp.
625 mL	all-purpose flour	2 1/2 cups
5 mL	baking powder	1 tsp.
5 mL	salt	1 tsp.

Utensils

mixing bowl
measuring cup and spoons
wooden spoon
rolling pin

cookie cutters
spatula
cookie sheet
wire rack

1. In a mixing bowl, cream together the shortening and sugar with a wooden spoon until light and smooth.

2. Add the eggs and vanilla. Beat until smooth.

3. Add the flour, baking powder and salt. Stir until well blended.

4. Cover the bowl with plastic wrap and refrigerate for 1 hour.

5. Heat the oven to 200°C (400°F).

6. Divide the dough into 4 pieces. On a lightly floured surface, roll out one piece at a time with a rolling pin until it is 3 mm (1/8 in.) thick. Keep the remaining dough chilled until you are ready to roll it.

7. Cut the dough with a cookie cutter. Lift the cookies with a spatula and place them on an ungreased cookie sheet 2.5 cm (1 in.) apart. Gather the scrap dough together and roll again. Repeat until all the dough has been used.

8. Bake the cookies, one cookie sheet at a time, for 6 to 8 minutes or until cookies are light brown. Remove the cookies from the cookie sheet using oven mitts and a spatula. Carefully place them on a wire rack to cool.

Helpful Hints

▷ Rub a little flour on the rolling pin to keep the dough from sticking to it.

▷ The thinner the dough, the crispier the cookies will be.

▷ To keep a cookie cutter from sticking, dip it in flour, then shake it before cutting.

**Level:
Intermediate**

**Makes:
16 brownies**

**Preparation:
10 to 15
minutes**

**Baking:
20 minutes**

**Cooling:
1 hour**

Brownies

For chocolate lovers, it doesn't get much better than this!

You Will Need

125 mL	butter or margarine	½ cup
125 mL	cocoa	½ cup
250 mL	brown sugar, firmly packed	1 cup
2	eggs	2
2 mL	vanilla	½ tsp.
125 mL	all-purpose flour	½ cup
125 mL	chopped walnuts (optional)	½ cup
2 mL	salt	½ tsp.

Utensils

20 cm (8 in.) square baking pan   saucepan
measuring cup and spoons   knife
wooden spoon

1. Heat the oven to 180°C (350°F). Grease a square pan.

2. Melt the butter in a saucepan. Remove from the heat.

3. Add the cocoa. Stir. Add brown sugar. Stir.

4. Add the eggs one at a time, stirring after each one. Add the vanilla and beat until blended.

5. Add flour, walnuts and salt. Stir.

6. Spread the batter evenly in the pan.

7. Bake for 20 minutes. Do not bake any longer. Let cool at least 1 hour before topping with Creamy Fudge Frosting and cutting into squares.

Creamy Fudge Frosting

1. Melt 25 mL (2 tbsp.) butter in a small saucepan. Remove from heat. Stir in 50 mL (¼ cup) cocoa.

2. While stirring, add 250 mL (1 cup) icing sugar and 2 mL (½ tsp.) vanilla. Continue stirring and slowly add 15–25 mL (1–2 tbsp.) milk until the frosting is smooth and creamy.

3. Spread evenly over brownies with a knife.

Level:
Beginner

Makes:
12 cupcakes

Preparation:
20 minutes

Baking:
20 minutes

Chocolate Mayonnaise Cupcakes

Serve these cupcakes with a huge scoop of whipped cream and chocolate sprinkles on top.

You Will Need

375 mL	all-purpose flour	1 1/2 cups
175 mL	sugar	3/4 cup
75 mL	cocoa	1/3 cup
6 mL	baking powder	1 1/4 tsp.
4 mL	baking soda	3/4 tsp.
175 mL	mayonnaise	3/4 cup
175 mL	water	3/4 cup
1	egg	1

Utensils

12-cup muffin tin
12 paper liners
large mixing bowl
small bowl
measuring cup and spoons

wooden spoon
whisk or fork
wire rack
toothpick

1. Heat the oven to 180°C (350°F). Line the muffin tin with paper liners.

2. In a large mixing bowl, stir together the flour, sugar, cocoa, baking powder and baking soda.

3. In a small bowl, combine the mayonnaise, water and egg. Beat well.

4. Add the wet ingredients to the flour mixture. Stir until just mixed.

5. Spoon the batter into the paper liners, filling each one about two-thirds full.

6. Bake for 20 minutes or until a toothpick inserted into the center of a cupcake comes out clean.

7. To remove the cupcakes from the pan, use oven mitts and turn the pan upside down over a wire rack. Set them right way up and let cool completely.

Try this!

▷ Add 175 mL (3/4 cup) chocolate chips for the ultimate delight.

▷ To make a cake, pour the batter into a greased 20 cm (8 in.) square pan and bake at 180°C (350°F) for 35 minutes or until a toothpick comes out clean when inserted into the center of the cake.

**Level:
Intermediate**

**Makes:
16 to 24
servings**

**Preparation:
30 minutes**

**Baking:
35 to 40
minutes**

Carrot Cake with Cream Cheese Icing

This moist cake isn't as sweet as some, but it's full of flavor — and healthy ingredients.

You Will Need

4	eggs, beaten	4
250 mL	sugar	1 cup
250 mL	vegetable oil	1 cup
250 mL	all-purpose flour	1 cup
250 mL	whole wheat flour	1 cup
10 mL	cinnamon	2 tsp.
7 mL	baking soda	1 1/2 tsp.
5 mL	salt	1 tsp.
500 mL	grated carrots	2 cups
375 mL	peeled and grated apples	1 1/2 cups
250 mL	raisins	1 cup
125 mL	chopped walnuts (optional)	1/2 cup

Utensils

measuring cup and spoons	grater
32 cm x 23 cm (13 in. x 9 in.) cake pan	fork
2 mixing bowls	large bowl
potato peeler	wooden spoon
skewer or toothpick	wire rack

1. Heat the oven to 180°C (350°F). Grease the cake pan. Put a little flour in it and shake it until the flour sticks to the bottoms and sides. Tip out any excess flour.

2. In a large mixing bowl, combine the eggs, sugar and vegetable oil. Beat with a fork until slightly thickened.

3. In another mixing bowl, combine both flours, cinnamon, baking soda and salt. Stir.

4. Add the flour mixture to the egg mixture. Stir.

5. Add the carrots, apples, raisins and nuts. Stir until blended.

6. Spoon the batter into the pan. Bake for 35 to 40 minutes or until a skewer or toothpick inserted in the center comes out clean. Let cool for at least 15 minutes, then turn out onto a wire rack.

7. After the cake has cooled completely, frost with Cream Cheese Icing.

Cream Cheese Icing

1. Place 125 g (4 oz.) cream cheese and 50 mL (¼ cup) soft butter in a large bowl. Beat until fluffy.

2. Add 250 mL (1 cup) icing sugar and 2 mL (1 tsp.) vanilla. Beat until well blended.

3. Spread the icing on the cooled carrot cake.

Level:
Intermediate

Makes:
6 servings

Preparation:
20 minutes

Baking:
45 minutes

Apple Upside-Down Cake

This cake is made upside down. What starts out as the bottom ends up on the top.

You Will Need

50 mL	butter or margarine	3 tbsp.
75 mL	brown sugar, firmly packed	1/3 cup
3	McIntosh apples	3
375 mL	all-purpose flour	1 1/2 cups
125 mL	sugar	1/2 cup
5 mL	baking powder	1 tsp.
5 mL	cinnamon	1 tsp.
2 mL	nutmeg	1/2 tsp.
1	egg	1
125 mL	milk	1/2 cup
75 mL	soft butter	1/3 cup
50 mL	molasses	1/4 cup

Utensils

large mixing bowl
measuring cup and spoons
22 cm (9 in.) round or square pan
toothpick or skewer
knife

paring knife
spatula
electric mixer
cookie sheet

1. Heat the oven to 180°C (350°F).

2. Place the butter in the cake pan. Put the pan in the oven just long enough to melt the butter.

3. Using oven mitts, remove the pan from oven. Stir in the brown sugar. Spread the mixture evenly over the bottom of the pan.

4. With a paring knife, peel, core and thinly slice the apples. Place the slices in a single layer over the bottom of the pan.

5. Combine the rest of the ingredients in a large mixing bowl. Beat with an electric mixer at medium speed for 2 minutes.

6. Spread batter evenly over the apples in the pan.

7. Place the pan in the oven on the top rack. Place a cookie sheet on the rack below in case the cake bubbles over. Bake for 45 minutes or until a toothpick inserted in the center comes out clean. Remove from the oven with oven mitts and immediately loosen cake from the edges of the pan with a knife.

8. Place a serving plate on top of the pan. Wearing oven mitts (and perhaps with some adult help), quickly flip the pan and plate upside down. The cake should fall onto the plate. Lift off the pan. If some of the apple mixture sticks to the bottom of the pan, just scoop it back in place.

9. Serve warm with whipped cream.

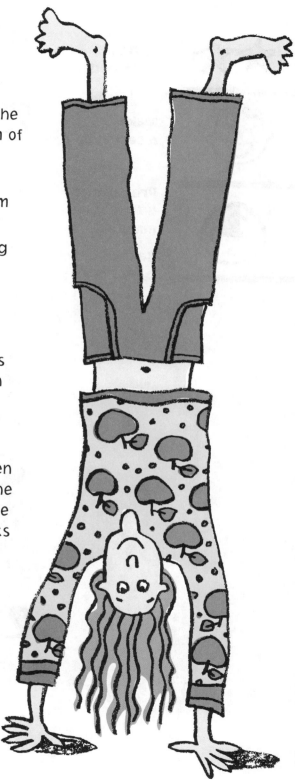

Level:
Intermediate

Makes:
6 servings

Preparation:
5 to 10 minutes

Baking:
2 1/2 hours

Rice Pudding

Another old-fashioned family favorite, comforting rice pudding also tastes great cold the next day.

You Will Need

125 mL	white or brown rice (uncooked)	1/2 cup
750 mL	milk	3 cups
125 mL	sugar	1/2 cup
5 mL	vanilla	1 tsp.
2 mL	nutmeg	1/2 tsp.
pinch	salt	pinch
2	egg yolks, beaten	2
50 mL	heavy (35%) cream	1/4 cup

Utensils

2 L (2 quart) casserole dish   wooden spoon
measuring cup and spoons   fork or whisk
small bowl
baking pan (large enough to hold the casserole dish)

1. Heat the oven to 160°C (325°F). Generously butter a casserole dish.

2. Put the rice in the casserole dish. Add the milk, sugar, vanilla, nutmeg and salt. Stir well.

3. Place the casserole dish in the baking pan. Fill the pan with cold water about 2.5 cm (1 in.) deep.

4. Bake for 1 ½ hours, stirring a few times in the first hour to keep the rice from sticking together.

5. In a small bowl, combine the egg yolks and cream. Beat well.

6. Using oven mitts, carefully remove the casserole dish from the oven. Add the egg mixture to the rice. Stir it in quickly.

7. Bake for another hour or until the rice is cooked and the pudding is set and lightly browned.

8. Serve warm or at room temperature.

✿ Try this!

▷ Add 125 mL (½ cup) raisins and 2 mL (½ tsp.) cinnamon when adding the eggs.

▷ Add 250 mL (1 cup) chopped dried fruit (such as dried apricots) when adding the eggs.

Level: Beginner

Makes: 6 servings

Preparation: 5 to 10 minutes

Cooking: 4 to 5 minutes

Chocolate Fondue

Try this fun dessert at a party.

You Will Need

	fresh fruit, cut into bite-sized pieces	
250 mL	semisweet chocolate chips	1 cup
250 mL	miniature marshmallows	1 cup
50 mL	milk	¼ cup

Utensils

serving plate   measuring cup
toothpicks   chef's knife
small glass casserole dish

1. Arrange the fruit pieces on a serving plate, and place a toothpick in each one.

2. Place the chocolate chips, marshmallows and milk in a small glass casserole dish.

3. Microwave uncovered on medium for 1 minute. Stir. Fondue will be very hot, so use oven mitts when removing the dish to stir. Repeat until the mixture comes to a full boil and is thick and smooth. If the mixture is too thick, add 5 mL (1 tsp.) of milk.

4. Using oven mitts, remove the dish from the microwave. Let cool for several minutes.

5. Place the bowl in the center of the fruit platter.

6. Each person spears chunks of fruit with toothpicks and dunks the pieces into the fondue.

7. If the fondue begins to cool, microwave on high for 2 minutes. Stir well. Be careful — it will be very hot again.

 **Try this!**

Dip whole strawberries into the hot chocolate. Let them cool on waxed paper. Once cool, strawberries will have a delicious chocolate coating. Refrigerate leftovers.

Drinks

Creamy Delights

Level:
Beginner

Makes:
2 servings

Preparation:
10 minutes

When you are in hurry, or just don't feel like eating a whole meal, whip up one of these fast meals in a glass. For all these recipes, just put everything in a blender (or a food processor) and whirl until smooth.

Blender Breakfast

You Will Need

250 mL	plain yogurt	1 cup
125 mL	orange or pineapple juice	1/2 cup
15 mL	honey (optional)	1 tbsp.
2 mL	vanilla	1/2 tsp.
1	large banana	1

Orange-Peach Shake

You Will Need

125 mL	orange juice	1 1/2 cup
125 mL	water	1/2 cup
125 mL	plain yogurt	1/2 cup
1	large peach, peeled and chopped	1

Banana-Pineapple Frostie

You Will Need

4	ice cubes	4
250 mL	chopped fresh or canned pineapple	1 cup
250 mL	plain yogurt	1 cup
1	large banana	1

Strawberry-Kiwi Smoothie

If kiwis are not in season, substitute one banana.

You Will Need

250 mL	chopped strawberries	1 cup
250 mL	peeled and chopped kiwi	1 cup
250 mL	plain yogurt	1 cup
125 mL	orange juice	1/2 cup

Tofu Smoothie

You Will Need

50 mL	silken tofu	3 tbsp.
4	ice cubes	4
1	large banana	1
6	strawberries	6
250 mL	soy milk	1 cup
125 mL	orange juice	1/2 cup

Tropical Tofu Frostie

You Will Need

50 mL	silken tofu	3 tbsp.
4	ice cubes	4
1	large banana	1
1	kiwi, peeled	1
250 mL	soy milk	1 cup
125 mL	pineapple juice	1/2 cup

⭐ Index

🥦 = vegan recipes